The Black Flag

Peter Kropotkin on Anarchism

by Peter Kropotkin

Red and Black Publishers, St Petersburg, Florida

Library of Congress Cataloging-in-Publication Data

Kropotkin, Petr Alekseevich, kniaz', 1842-1921.
    The black flag : Peter Kropotkin on anarchism / by Peter Kropotkin.
        p. cm.
    ISBN 978-1-934941-81-2
1. Anarchism. 2. Anarchism--History. 3. Communism. I. Title.
    HX883.K76 2010
    335'.83--dc22

                                                    2010007746

Red and Black Publishers, PO Box 7542, St Petersburg, Florida, 33734
Contact us at: info@RedandBlackPublishers.com
        Printed and manufactured in the United States of America

Contents

Editor's Preface

Peter Kropotkin was born in Moscow in December 1842, the son of a Russian Tsarist nobleman who owned vast tracts of land and over 1000 serfs. While a young boy, he became interested in the condition of the peasant serfs, and at the age of 12, he ceased referring to himself as "Prince", and demanded others stop using the title to refer to him. In 1857, the 15-year old Kropotkin traveled to St Petersburg to attend a military school for the children of nobility. During this time, he began to read translated versions of French revolutionary pamphlets. They would have a huge effect on him.

After graduating from military school, Kropotkin joined a regiment of Cossacks in a largely unexplored Amur region in Siberia. Although Kropotkin had no interest in a military career, the posting gave him the opportunity to lead several scientific and exploratory expeditions in the area.

In 1867, Kropotkin quit the Army and entered St Petersburg University to study geology. As an official in the Russian Geographical Society, he led expeditions to Finland, Sweden, and across Russia.

In 1872, during a trip to Switzerland, Kropotkin came into contact with Karl Marx's International Workingmen's Association, and his interest in radical politics was rekindled. Distrusting the centralized structure of the International, Kropotkin turned to anarchism instead, and met with members of the Jura Federation. When he returned to

Russia, he joined the Circle of Tchaikovsky, a Russian anarchist group. Arrested for anarchist activities, Kropotkin escaped from prison in 1876 and made his way to England, then returned to Switzerland to join the Jura Federation.

After Tsar Alaexander II was assassinated in 1881 by revolutionaries, the Russian government put diplomatic pressure on Switzerland to expel its Russian exiles, and Kropotkin was deported. After a short stay in London, Kropotkin went to France, where he was arrested, only to be released in 1886. He returned to London, where he continued to write anarchist pamphlets and books.

After the 1917 February Revolution in Russia, Kropotkin returned to Moscow and was offered the position of Minister of Education in Kerensky's Provisional Government, but turned it down. When the Bolsheviks took power in November 1917, Kropotkin became an outspoken critic. Although the Leninists ruthlessly jailed anarchists, Kropotkin's popularity protected him. He died in February 1921.

Revolutionary Government

1880

(Editor's Note: In this pamphlet, Kropotkin, anarchism's best-known and most prolific theoretician, spells out the essential difference between anarchism and all the other radical social movements – the uncompromising demand that all hierarchical state structures, even a socialist one, be destroyed.)

That the governments existing at present ought to be abolished, so that liberty, equality, and fraternity should no longer be empty words but become living realities, and that all forms of government as yet tried have only been so many forms of oppression and ought to be replaced by a new form of grouping, will be agreed by all who have a brain and a temperament ever so little revolutionary. One does not need to be much of an innovator to arrive at this conclusion. The vices of the governments today and the impossibility of reforming them are too evident to be hidden from the eyes of any reasonable observer. And as for overturning governments, it is well known that at certain epochs that can be done without much difficulty. There are times when governments crumble to pieces almost of themselves like a house of cards, before the breath of the people in revolt.

To overturn a government – is for a revolutionary middle-class man everything; for us it is only the beginning of the social revolution. The machine of the State once out of gear, the hierarchy of functionaries disorganized and not knowing in what direction to take a step, the soldiers having lost confidence in their officers—in a word, the whole army of defenders of the capital once routed—then it is that the grand work of destruction of all the institutions which serve to perpetuate economic and political slavery will become ours. The possibility of acting freely being attained, what will revolutionists do next?

To this question the anarchists alone give the proper answer: "No Government!" All the others say "A Revolutionary Government!" and they differ only as to the form to be given to that government. Some decide for a government elected by universal suffrage in the state or in the commune; others decide on a revolutionary dictatorship.

A revolutionary government! There are two words which sound very strange in the ears of those who really understand what the social revolution means, and what government means. The words contradict each other, destroy each other. We have seen, of course, many despotic governments—it is the essence of all government to take the side of the reaction against the revolution, and we have a tendency towards despotism. But such a thing as a revolutionary government has never been seen, and the reason is that the revolution—meaning the demolition by violence of the established forms of property, the destruction of castes, the rapid transformation of received ideas about morality, is precisely the opposite, the very negation of government, this being the synonym of "established order", of conservatism, of the maintenance of existing institutions, the negation of free initiative and individual action. And yet we continually hear this white blackbird spoken of as if a "revolutionary government" were the simplest thing in the world, as common and as well known to all as royalty, the empire, and the papacy!

That the so-called revolutionists of the middle class should preach this idea is nothing strange. We know well what they understand by "revolution". They understand by it a bolstering up of their republic, the taking possession by the so-called republicans of the lucrative employments reserved today for the royalists. It means at the most the divorce of church and state, replaced by the concubinage of the two, the sequestration of goods of the clergy for the benefit of the State, and above all for that of the future administrators of these goods. Perhaps it may mean the referendum, or some other political machinery. But that revolutionary socialists should make themselves the apostles of such an idea can only be explained by supposing one of two things. Either they are imbued with prejudices which they have imbibed without knowing it from literature, and above all from history written to suit the middle-class ideas; or else they do not really desire this revolution which they have always on their lips. They would be content with the simple plastering up of the present institutions, provided that they would secure power for themselves, leaving to the future to decide what they should do to satisfy "the beast" called "the people". They only go against the governors of the present time in order to take their places. With these people we do not care to argue. We will therefore only speak to those who honestly deceive themselves.

Let us begin with the first of the forms of "revolutionary government" which is advocated — the elected government.

The power of the royalty we will suppose has just been overturned, the army of defenders of capital is routed; everywhere there is fermentation, discussion of public affairs, everywhere a desire to march onward. New ideas arise, the necessity of important changes is perceived. It is necessary to act, it is necessary to begin without pity the work of demolition in order to prepare the ground for new life. But what do they propose to us to do? To convoke the people to elections, to elect at once a government and confide to it the work which all of us, and each of us, should undertake of our own initiative.

This is what Paris did after the 18th of March 1871. "I will never forget," said a friend to us, "those delightful moments of deliverance. I came down from my upper chamber in the Latin Quarter to join that immense open-air club which filled the boulevards from one end of Paris to the other. Everyone talked about public affairs; all mere personal preoccupations were forgotten; no more was thought of buying or selling; all felt ready, body and soul, to advance towards the future. Men of the middle-class even, carried away by the general enthusiasm, saw with joy a new world open up. 'If it is necessary to make a social revolution,' they said, 'make it then. Put all things in common; we are ready for it.' All the elements of revolution were there, it was only necessary to set them to work. When I returned to my lodging at night I said to myself, 'How fine is humanity after all, but no one knew it; it has always been calumniated.' Then came the elections, the members of the commune were named and then little by little the ardor of devotion and the desire for action were extinguished. Everyone returned to his usual task, saying to himself, 'Now we have an honest government, let it act for us.'" What followed everyone knows.

Instead of acting for themselves, instead of marching forward, instead of advancing in the direction of the new order of things, the people confiding in their governors, entrusted to them the charge of taking initiative. This was the first consequence of the inevitable result of elections. Let us see now what these governors did who were invested with the confidence of all.

Never were elections more fierce than those of March, 1871. The opponents of the commune admit it themselves. Never was the great mass of electors more influenced with the desire to place in power the best men, men of the future, true revolutionists. And so they did. All well known revolutionists were elected by immense majorities: Jacobins, Blanquists, Internationalists, all three revolutionary divisions were represented in the council of the commune. No election could give a better government.

But what was the result? Shut up in the city hall, charged to proceed after the forms established by the preceding governments, these ardent revolutionists, these reformers, found themselves smitten with incapacity and sterility. With all their good will and their courage they did not even know how to organize a defense of Paris. Of course people now blame the men, the individuals for this; but it was not the men who were the cause for this failure—it was the system.

In fact, universal suffrage, when it is quite free, can only produce, at best, an assembly which represents the average of the opinions which at the time are held by the mass of the people. And this average at the outbreak of the revolution has only a vague idea of the work to be accomplished, without understanding at all how they ought to undertake it. Ah, if the bulk of the nation, of the commune, could only understand before the movement what is necessary to be done as soon as the government is overturned! If this dream of the utopians of the chair could be realized, we never would have had bloody revolutions. The will of the bulk of the nation once expressed, the rest would submit to it with a good grace, but this is not how things are done. The revolution bursts out long before a general understanding has come, and those who have a clear idea of what should be done the next day are only a very small minority. The great mass of the people have as yet only a general idea of the end which they wish realized, without knowing much how to advance towards that end, and without having much confidence in the direction to follow. The practical solution will not be found, will not be made clear until the change will have already begun. It will be the product of the revolution itself, of the people in action—or else it will be nothing, the brain of a few individuals being absolutely incapable of finding solutions which can only spring from the life of the people.

This is the situation which is reflected in the body elected by universal suffrage, even if it had not the vices inherent in representative governments in general. The few men who represent the revolutionary idea of the epoch find themselves swamped among the representatives of the revolutionary schools of the past, and the existing order of things. These men who would be so necessary among the people, particularly in the days of the revolution, to sow broadcast their ideas, to put the mass in movement, to demolish the institutions of the past, find themselves shut up in a hall, vainly discussing how to wrest concessions from the moderates, and how to convert their enemies, while there is really only one way of inducing them to accept the new idea—namely, to put it into execution. The government becomes a parliament with all the vices of a middle-class parliament. Far from being a "revolutionary" government it becomes the greatest obstacle to the revolution and at last the people find themselves compelled to put it out of the way, to dismiss those that but yesterday they acclaimed as their chosen.

But it is not so easy to do so. The new government, which has hastened to organize a new administration in order to extend its domination and make itself obeyed, does not understand giving up so easily. Jealous of maintaining its power, it clings to it with all the energy of an institution which has not yet had time to fall into senile decay. It decides to oppose force with force, and there is only one means then to dislodge it, namely, to take up arms, to make another revolution in order to dismiss those in whom the people had placed all their hopes.

There you see the revolution divided against itself! After losing precious time in delays, it now loses its strength in internecine divisions between friends of the new government and those who see necessity of dissolving it. And all this happens because it has not been understood that a new life requires new forms; that it is not by clinging to ancient forms that a revolution can be carried out! All this for not having understood the incompatibility of revolution and government, for not having seen that one is, under whatever form it presents itself, the negation of the other, and that outside of anarchism there is no such thing as revolution.

It is just the same with regard to that other form of "revolutionary government" so often extolled — a revolutionary dictatorship.

Dictatorship

The dangers to which the revolution is exposed when it allows itself to be controlled by an elected government are so evident that a whole school of revolutionists entirely renounces the idea of it. They understand that it is impossible for a people in insurrection to give themselves, by means of elections, any government but the one that represents the past, and which must be like leaden shoes on the feet of the people, above all when it is necessary to accomplish that immense regeneration, economic, political, and moral, which we understand by the social revolution. They renounce then the idea of "legal" government at least during the period which is a revolt against legality, and they advocate "revolutionary dictatorship".

"The party", say they, "which will have overturned the government will take the place of it, of course. It will seize upon power and proceed in a revolutionary manner. It will take the measures necessary to secure the success of the insurrection. It will demolish the old institutions; it will organize the defense of the country. As for those who will not recognize its authority, why the guillotine will settle them, whether they belong to the people or the middle-class, if they refuse to obey the orders necessary for the advance of the revolution." The guillotine still in action? See how these budding Robespierres argue, who know nothing of the grand epic of the century but its period of decline, men who have never learned anything about it except from speeches of hangers-on of the Republic.

For us anarchists the dictatorship of an individual or of a party (at bottom the very same thing) has been finally condemned. We know that revolution and government are incompatible. One must destroy the other no matter what name is given to government, whether dictatorship, royalty, or parliament. We know that what makes the strength and the truth of our party is contained in this formula — "Nothing good or durable can be done except by the free initiative of the people, and every government tends to destroy it." And so the very best among us, if they should become masters of that formidable machine, the government, would become, in a week, fit only for the gallows, if their ideas had not to pass through the crucible of the popular mind before being put into execution. We know whither every dictatorship leads, even the best intentioned — namely, to the death of the revolutionary movement. We know also, that this idea of dictatorship is never anything more than a sickly product of governmental fetish worship, which, like religious fetish-worship, has always served to perpetuate slavery.

But we do not address ourselves to anarchists. We speak to those governmental revolutionists who, led astray by prejudices of their education, honestly deceive themselves, and ask nothing better than to discuss the question. We therefore speak to them from their own point-of-view.

To begin with one general observation: those who preach dictatorship do not in general perceive that in sustaining this prejudice they only prepare the way for those who later on will cut their throats. There is, however, one word of Robespierre's which his admirers would do well to remember. He did not deny the dictatorship in principle; but "have good care about it," he answered abruptly to Mandar when he spoke to him of it, "Brissot would be the dictator!" Yes, Brissot, the crafty Girondin, deadly enemy of the leveling tendencies of the people, furious defender of property (although he called it theft), Brissot, who would coolly have consigned to the Abbaye Prison, Hérbert, Marat, and all the moderate Jacobins!

Now this was said in 1792! At that time France had already been three years in revolution! In fact royalty no longer existed, it only awaited its death stroke. The feudal regime was actually abolished. And yet even at this time when the revolution rolled its waves untrammeled, it was still the counter-revolutionist Brissot who had the best chance to be made dictator! And who would it have been previously, in 1789? Mirabeau is the man who would have been acknowledged as the head of government! The man who made a bargain with the king to sell him his eloquence, this is the man who would have been thrust into power at this time, if the insurgent people had not imposed its sovereignty, sustained by its pikes, and if it had not provided by the accomplished facts of *jacquerie*, in making illusory every government constituted at Paris or in the departments.

But governmental prejudice so thoroughly blinds those who speak of dictatorship, that they prefer the dictatorship of a new Brissot or a Napoleon to abandoning the idea of giving another master to men who are breaking the chains of slavery.

The secret societies of the time of the restoration and the Louis-Philippe contributed powerfully to maintain this prejudice of dictatorship. The middle-class republicans of the time, aided by workers, made a long series of conspiracies, with the object of overturning royalty and proclaiming the republic. Not understanding the profound change that would have to be effected in France before even a republican régime could be established, they imagined that by means of vast conspiracy they would someday overturn royalty, take possession of power and proclaim the Republic. For more than thirty years those secret societies never ceased to work with an unlimited devotion and heroic courage and perseverance. If the republic resulted from the insurrection of 1848, it was thanks to these societies, and thanks to the propaganda by deed made by them for thirty years. Without their noble efforts the republic would have been impossible.

The end they had in view was to get possession of power themselves and to install a republican dictatorship. But of course they never succeeded. As ever, from the nature of things, a conspiracy could not overturn royalty. The conspirators had indeed prepared the way for its fall. They had spread widely the republican idea; their martyrs had made it the ideal of the people. But the final effort which definitely overturned the king of the bourgeoisie was much greater and stronger than any that could come from a secret society; it came from the mass of the people.

The result is known. The party which had prepared the way for the fall of royalty found itself thrust aside from the steps of the government house. Others, too prudent to run the risk of conspiracy, but better known, more moderate also, lying in wait for the opportunity of grasping power, took the place which the conspirators hoped to conquer at the point of the bayonet. Journalists, lawyers, good talkers who worked hard to make a name for themselves while the true republicans forged weapons or expired in prison, took possession of power. Some of them, already well known, were acclaimed by the people; others pushed themselves forward and were accepted because their name represented nothing more than a program of agreement with everybody.

It is useless to tell us that this happened because of a want of practical spirit in the party of action, and that others will be able to do better in the future. No, a thousand times no! It is a law as immutable as that which governs the movement of the stars, that the party of action must be thrown aside, and the intriguers and the talkers seize upon power. They are always better known to the great mass that makes the final effort. They get more votes, because with or without voting papers, by acclamation or by the ballot box, at the bottom it is always a kind of tacit election which is made in such cases by acclamation. They are acclaimed by everybody and above all by the enemies of the revolution, who prefer to put forward nobodies, and thus by acclamation those men are accepted as rulers who are really either enemies of the movement or indifferent toward it.

The man who more than any other was the incarnation of this system of conspiracy, the man who by a life spent in prison paid for his devotion to this system on the eve of his death uttered these words, which of themselves make an entire program — "Neither God nor Master!"

The Impotence Of Revolutionary Government

To imagine that a government can be overturned by a secret society, and that secret society can take its place, is an error into which have fallen all the revolutionary organizations which sprang to life in the bosom of the republican middle-class since 1820. And yet facts abound which prove what an error it is. What devotion, what abnegation, what perseverance was not displayed by the republican secret societies of the young Italy party! And yet all this immense work, all these sacrifices made by the youth of Italy, before which even those of the Russian revolutionary youth pale, all the corpses piled up in the casemates of Austrian fortresses, and under knife and bullets of the executioner — all this only brought into power the crafty, robbing middle class and royalty!

It is inevitable, it cannot be otherwise. For it is not secret societies nor even revolutionary organizations that can give the finishing blow governments. Their function, their historic mission, is to prepare men's minds for the revolution, and then when men's minds are prepared and external circumstances are favorable, the final rush is made, not by the group that initiated the movement, but by the mass of the people altogether outside of the society. On the 31st of August Paris was deaf to the appeals of Blanqui. Four days later he proclaimed the fall of the government; but then the blanquists were no longer the initiators of the movement. It was the people, the millions who dethroned the man of December and proclaimed the humbugs whose names for two years had resounded in their ears. When a revolution is ready to burst out, when a movement is felt in the air, when its success is already certain, then a thousand new men, on whom the organization has never exercised any direct influence, come and join the movement like birds of prey coming to the fields of battle to feed on the victims. These help to make the final effort, but it is not in the ranks of sincere irreconcilable conspirators, it is among the men on the fence that they look for their leaders. The conspirators who still are possessed with the prejudice of a dictatorship then unconsciously work to put into power their own enemies.

But if all this that we have just said is true with regard to political revolutions or rather outbreaks, it is much more true with regard to the revolution we desire — the social revolution. To allow any government to be established, a strong and recognized power, is to paralyze the work of the revolution at once. The good that this government would do is nil, and the evil immense.

What do we understand by "revolution"? It is not a simple change of governors. It is the taking possession by the people of all social wealth. It is the abolition of all forces which have so long hampered the development of humanity. But is it by decrees emanating from a government that this immense economic revolution be accomplished? We have seen in the past century the Polish revolutionary dictator Kosciusko decree the abolition of personal servitude, yet the servitude continued to exist for thirty years after this decree. We have seen the convention, the omnipotent convention, the terrible convention as its admirers call it, decree the equal division per head of all communal lands taken back from the nobles. Like so many others, this decree remained a dead letter because in order to carry it out it was necessary that the proletarians of the rural districts should make an entirely new revolution, and revolutions are not made by the force of decrees. In order that the taking possession of social wealth should become an accomplished fact it is necessary that the people should have their hands free, that they should shake off slavery to which they are too much habituated, that they act according to their own will, and march forward without waiting for orders from anyone. And it is this very thing which a dictatorship would prevent, however well intentioned it might be, while it would be incapable of advancing in the slightest degree the march of the revolution.

But if government, were it even an ideal revolutionary government, creates no new force and is of no use whatever in work of demolition which we have to accomplish, still less can we count on it for the work of reorganization which must follow that of demolition. The economic change which will result from the social revolution will be so immense and so profound, it must change all the relations based today on property and exchange, that it is impossible for one or any individual to elaborate the different social forms which must spring up in the society of the future. This elaboration of new social forms can only be made by the collective work of the masses. To satisfy the immense variety of conditions and needs which will spring up as soon as private property shall be abolished, it is necessary to have the collective suppleness of mind of the whole people. Any authority external to it will only be an obstacle, and beside that a source of discord and hatred.

But it is full time to give up this illusion, so often proved false and so often dearly paid for, of a "revolutionary government". It is time to admit, once for all, this political axiom that a government cannot be revolutionary. People talk of the convention, but let us not forget that a few measures taken by the convention, little revolutionary though they were, were only the sanction of action accomplished by the people who at the time trampled under foot all governments. As Victor Hugo had said, Danton pushed forward Robespierre, Marat watched and pushed on Dalton, and Marat himself was pushed on by Cimourdain – this personification of the clubs of wild enthusiasts and rebels. Like all governments that preceded it and followed it, the convention was only a drag on the action of the people.

The facts which history teach us are so conclusive in this respect, the impossibility of a revolutionary government and the injurious effect of that which is called by the name are so evident, that it would seem difficult to explain the determination with which a certain school calling itself socialist maintains the idea of government. But the explanation is very simple. It is that socialists, though they say they are followers of this school, have an entirely different conception from ours of the revolution which we have to accomplish. For them, as for all middle-class radicals, the social revolution is rather an affair of the future about which we have not to think much at present. What they dream of in their inmost thoughts, though they don't dare to confess it, is something entirely different. It is the installation of government like that of Switzerland or the United States, making some attempts at expropriation, in favor of the State, of what they call "public services". It is something after the ideal of Bismarck. It is a compromise made in advance between the socialistic aspirations of the masses and the desires of the middle class. They would, indeed, wish the expropriation to be complete, but they have not the courage to attempt it; so they put it off to the next century, and before the battle they enter into negotiation with the enemy.

Peter Kropotkin, 1880

Anarchist Communism: Its Basis and Principles

1887

(Editor's Note: In contrast to the previous pamphlet, which emphasizes the differences between socialism and anarchism, this pamphlet emphasizes the similarities. Like the socialists, anarchists want to destroy capitalism and replace it with a communalist economic structure.)

I

Anarchism, the no-government system of socialism, has a double origin. It is an outgrowth of the two great movements of thought in the economic and the political fields which characterise the nineteenth century, and especially its second part. In common with all socialists, the anarchists hold that the private ownership of land, capital, and machinery has had its time; that it is condemned to disappear; and that all requisites for production must, and will, become the common property of society, and be managed in common by the producers of wealth. And in common with the most advanced representatives of political radicalism, they maintain that the ideal of the political organisation of society is a condition of things where the functions of government are reduced to a minimum, and the individual recovers his full liberty of initiative and action for satisfying, by means of free groups and federations—freely constituted—all the infinitely varied needs of the human being.

As regards socialism, most of the anarchists arrive at its ultimate conclusion, that is, at a complete negation of the wage-system and at communism. And with reference to political organisation, by giving a further development to the above-mentioned part of the radical program, they arrive at the conclusion that the ultimate aim of society is the reduction of the functions of government to nil—that is, to a society without government, to an-archy. The anarchists maintain, moreover, that such being the ideal of social and political organisation, they must not remit it to future centuries, but that only those changes in our social organisation which are in accordance with the above double ideal, and constitute an approach to it, will have a chance of life and be beneficial for the commonwealth.

As to the method followed by the anarchist thinker, it entirely differs from that followed by the utopists. The anarchist thinker does not resort to metaphysical conceptions (like "natural rights," the "duties of the State," and so on) to establish what are, in his opinion, the best conditions for realising the greatest happiness of humanity. He follows, on the contrary, the course traced by the modern philosophy of evolution. He studies human society as it is now and was in the past; and without either endowing humanity as a whole, or separate individuals, with superior qualities which they do not possess, he merely considers society as an aggregation of organisms trying to find out the best ways of combining the wants of the individual with those of cooperation for the welfare of the species. He studies society and tries to discover its tendencies, past and present, its growing needs, intellectual and economic, and in his ideal he merely points out in which direction evolution goes. He distinguishes between the real wants and tendencies of human aggregations and the accidents (want of knowledge, migrations, wars, conquests) which have prevented these tendencies from being satisfied. And he concludes that the two most prominent, although often unconscious, tendencies throughout our history have been: first, a tendency towards integrating labour for the production of all riches in common, so as finally to render it impossible to discriminate the part of the common production due to the separate individual; and second, a tendency towards the fullest freedom of the individual in the prosecution of all aims, beneficial both for himself and for society at large. The ideal of the anarchist is thus a mere summing-up of what he considers to be the next phase of evolution. It is no longer a matter of faith; it is a matter for scientific discussion.

In fact, one of the leading features of this century is the growth of socialism and the rapid spreading of socialist views among the working-classes. How could it be otherwise? We have witnessed an unparalleled sudden increase of our powers of production, resulting in an accumulation of wealth which has outstripped the most sanguine expectations. But owing to our wage system, this increase of wealth — due to the combined efforts of men of science, of managers, and workmen as well — has resulted only in an unprecedented accumulation of wealth in the hands of the owners of capital; while an increase of misery for great numbers, and an insecurity of life for all, have been the lot of the workmen. The unskilled labourers, in continuous search for labour, are falling into an unheard-of destitution. And even the best paid artisans and skilled workmen labour under the permanent menace of being thrown, in their turn, into the same conditions as the unskilled paupers, in consequence of some of the continuous and unavoidable fluctuations of industry and caprices of capital.

The chasm between the modern millionaire who squanders the produce of human labour in a gorgeous and vain luxury, and the pauper reduced to a miserable and insecure existence, is thus growing wider and wider, so as to break the very unity of society — the harmony of its life — and to endanger the progress of its further development.

At the same time, workingmen are less and less inclined to patiently endure this division of society into two classes, as they themselves become more and more conscious of the wealth-producing power of modern industry, of the part played by labour in the production of wealth, and of their own capacities of organisation. In proportion as all classes of the community take a more lively part in public affairs, and knowledge spreads among the masses, their longing for equality becomes stronger, and their demands for social reorganisation become louder and louder. They can be ignored no more. The worker claims his share in the riches he produces; he claims his share in the management of production; and he claims not only some additional well-being, but also his full rights in the higher enjoyments of science and art. These claims, which formerly were uttered only by the social reformer, begin now to be made by a daily growing minority of those who work in the factory or till the acre. And they so conform to our feelings of justice that they find support in a daily growing minority among the privileged classes themselves. Socialism becomes thus the idea of the nineteenth century; and neither coercion nor pseudo-reforms can stop its further growth.

Much hope of improvement was placed, of course, in the extension of political rights to the working classes. But these concessions, unsupported as they were by corresponding changes in economic relations, proved delusions. They did not materially improve the conditions of the great bulk of the workmen. Therefore, the watchword of socialism is: "Economic freedom as the only secure basis for political freedom." And as long as the present wage system, with all its bad consequences, remains unaltered, the socialist watchword will continue to inspire the workmen. Socialism will continue to grow until it has realised its program.

Side by side with this great movement of thought in economic matters, a like movement has been going on with regard to political rights, political organisation, and the functions of government. Government has been submitted to the same criticism as capital. While most of the radicals saw in universal suffrage and republican institutions the last word of political wisdom, a further step was made by the few. The very functions of government and the State, as also their relations to the individual, were submitted to a sharper and deeper criticism. Representative government having been tried by experiment on a wide field, its defects became more and more prominent. It became obvious that these defects are not merely accidental but inherent in the system itself. Parliament and its executive proved to be unable to attend to all the numberless affairs of the community and to conciliate the varied and often opposite interests of the separate parts of a State. Election proved unable to find out the men who might represent a nation, and manage, otherwise than in a party spirit, the affairs they are compelled to legislate upon. These defects become so striking that the very principles of the representative system were criticised and their justness doubted.

Again, the dangers of a centralised government became still more conspicuous when the socialists came to the front and asked for a further increase of the powers of government by entrusting it with the management of the immense field covered now by the economic relations between individuals. The question was asked whether a government entrusted with the management of industry and trade would not become a permanent danger for liberty and peace, and whether it even would be able to be a good manager?

The socialists of the earlier part of this century did not fully realise the immense difficulties of the problem. Convinced as they were of the necessity of economic reforms, most of them took no notice of the need of freedom for the individual. And we have had social reformers ready to submit society to any kind of theocracy, or dictatorship, in order to obtain reforms in a socialist sense. Therefore we have seen in England and also on the Continent the division of men of advanced opinions into political radicals and socialists — the former looking with distrust on the latter, as they saw in them a danger for the political liberties which have been won by the civilised nations after a long series of struggles. And even now, when the socialists all over Europe have become political parties, and profess the democratic faith, there remains among most impartial men a well-founded fear of the *Volksstaat* or "popular State" being as great a danger to liberty as any form of autocracy if its government be entrusted with the management of all the social organisation including the production and distribution of wealth.

Recent evolution, however, has prepared the way for showing the necessity and possibility of a higher form of social organisation which may guarantee economic freedom without reducing the individual to the role of a slave to the State. The origins of government have been carefully studied, and all metaphysical conceptions as to its divine or "social contract" derivation having been laid aside, it appears that it is among us of a relatively modern origin, and that its powers have grown precisely in proportion as the division of society into the privileged and unprivileged classes was growing in the course of ages. Representative government has also been reduced to its real value — that of an instrument which has rendered services in the struggle against autocracy, but not an ideal of free political organisation. As to the system of philosophy which saw in the State a leader of progress, it was more and more shaken as it became evident that progress is the most effective when it is not checked by State interference. It has thus become obvious that a further advance in social life does not lie in the direction of a further concentration of power and regulative functions in the hands of a governing body, but in the direction of decentralisation, both territorial and functional — in a subdivision of public functions with respect both to their sphere of action and to the character of the functions; it is in the abandonment to the initiative of freely constituted groups of all those functions which are now considered as the functions of government.

This current of thought has found its expression not merely in literature, but also to a limited extent in life. The uprise of the Paris Commune, followed by that of the Commune of Cartagena—a movement of which the historical bearing seems to have been quite overlooked—opened a new page of history. If we analyse not only this movement in itself, but also the impression it left in the minds and the tendencies manifested during the communal revolution, we must recognise in it an indication showing that in the future human agglomerations which are more advanced in their social development will try to start an independent life; and that they will endeavour to convert the more backward parts of a nation by example, instead of imposing their opinions by law and force, or submitting themselves to the majority-rule, which always is a mediocrity-rule. At the same time the failure of representative government within the Commune itself proved that self-government and self-administration must be carried further than in a merely territorial sense. To be effective they must also be carried into the various functions of life within the free community. A merely territorial limitation of the sphere of action of government will not do—representative government being as deficient in a city as it is in a nation. Life gave thus a further point in favour of the no-government theory, and a new impulse to anarchist thought.

Anarchists recognise the justice of both the just-mentioned tendencies towards economic and political freedom, and see in them two different manifestations of the very same need of equality which constitutes the very essence of all struggles mentioned by history. Therefore, in common with all socialists, the anarchist says to the political reformer: "No substantial reform in the sense of political equality and no limitation of the powers of government can be made as long as society is divided into two hostile camps, and the labourer remains, economically speaking, a slave to his employer." But to the state socialist we say also: "You cannot modify the existing conditions of property without deeply modifying at the same time the political organisation. You must limit the powers of government and renounce parliamentary rule. To each new economic phase of life corresponds a new political phase. Absolute monarchy corresponded to the system of serfdom. Representative government corresponds to capital-rule. Both, however, are class-rule. But in a society where the distinction between capitalist and labourer has disappeared, there is no need of such a government; it would be an anachronism, a nuisance. Free workers would require a free organisation, and this cannot have any other basis than free agreement and free cooperation, without sacrificing the autonomy of the individual to the all-pervading interference of the State. The no-capitalist system implies the no-government system."

Meaning thus the emancipation of man from the oppressive powers of capitalism and government as well, the system of anarchism becomes a synthesis of the two powerful currents of thought which characterise our century.

In arriving at these conclusions, anarchism proves to be in accordance with the conclusions arrived at by the philosophy of evolution. By bringing to light the plasticity of organisation, the philosophy of evolution has shown the admirable adaptability of organisms to their conditions of life, and the ensuing development of such faculties as render more complete both the adaptations of the aggregates to their surroundings and those of each of the constituent parts of the aggregate to the needs of free cooperation. It has familiarised us with the circumstance that throughout organic nature the capacities for life in common grow in proportion as the integration of organisms into compound aggregates becomes more and more complete; and it has enforced thus the opinion already expressed by social moralists as to the perfectibility of human nature. It has shown us that, in the long run of the struggle for existence, "the fittest" will prove to be those who combine intellectual knowledge with the knowledge necessary for the production of wealth, and not those who are now the richest because they, or their ancestors, have been momentarily the strongest.

By showing that the "struggle for existence" must be conceived not merely in its restricted sense of a struggle between individuals for the means of subsistence but in its wider sense of adaptation of all individuals of the species to the best conditions for the survival of the species, as well as for the greatest possible sum of life and happiness for each and all, it has permitted us to deduce the laws of moral science from the social needs and habits of mankind. It has shown us the infinitesimal part played by positive law in moral evolution, and the immense part played by the natural growth of altruistic feelings, which develop as soon as the conditions of life favour their growth. It has thus enforced the opinion of social reformers as to the necessity of modifying the conditions of life for improving man, instead of trying to improve human nature by moral teachings while life works in an opposite direction. Finally, by studying human society from the biological point of view, it has come to the conclusions arrived at by anarchists from the study of history and present tendencies as to further progress being in the line of socialisation of wealth and integrated labour combined with the fullest possible freedom of the individual.

It has happened in the long run of ages that everything which permits men to increase their production, or even to continue it, has been appropriated by the few. The land, which derives its value precisely from its being necessary for an ever-increasing population, belongs to the few, who may prevent the community from cultivating it. The coal-pits, which represent the labour of generations, and which also derive their value from the wants of the manufacturers and railroads, from the immense trade carried on and the density of population, belong again to the few, who have even the right of stopping the extraction of coal if they choose to give another use to their capital. The lace-weaving machine, which represents, in its present state of perfection, the work of three generations of Lancashire weavers, belongs also to the few; and if the grandsons of the very same weaver who invented the first lace-weaving machine claim their right to bring one of these machines into motion, they will be told "Hands off! This machine does not belong to you!" The railroads, which mostly would be useless heaps of iron if not for the present dense population, its industry, trade, and traffic, belong again to the few — to a few shareholders, who may not even know where the railway is situated which brings them a yearly income larger than that of a medieval king. And if the children of those people who died by thousands in digging the tunnels should gather and go — a ragged and starving crowd — to ask bread or work from the shareholders, they would be met with bayonets and bullets.

Who is the sophist who will dare to say that such an organisation is just? But what is unjust cannot be beneficial to mankind; and it is not. In consequence of this monstrous organisation, the son of a workman, when he is able to work, finds no acre to till, no machine to set in motion, unless he agrees to sell his labour for a sum inferior to its real value. His father and grandfather have contributed to drain the field, or erect the factory, to the full extent of their capacities—and nobody can do more than that—but he comes into the world more destitute than a savage. If he resorts to agriculture, he will be permitted to cultivate a plot of land, but on the condition that he gives up part of his product to the landlord. If he resorts to industry, he will be permitted to work, but on the condition that out of the thirty shillings he has produced, ten shillings or more will be pocketed by the owner of the machine. We cry out against the feudal barons who did not permit anyone to settle on the land otherwise than on payment of one quarter of the crops to the lord of the manor; but we continue to do as they did—we extend their system. The forms have changed, but the essence has remained the same. And the workman is compelled to accept the feudal conditions which we call "free contract," because nowhere will he find better conditions. Everything has been appropriated by somebody; he must accept the bargain, or starve.

Owing to this circumstance our production takes a wrong turn. It takes no care of the needs of the community; its only aim is to increase the profits of the capitalist. And we have, therefore—the continuous fluctuations of industry, the crisis coming periodically nearly every ten years, and throwing out of employment several hundred thousand men who are brought to complete misery, whose children grow up in the gutter, ready to become inmates of the prison and workhouse. The workmen being unable to purchase with their wages the riches they are producing, industry must search for markets elsewhere, amidst the middle classes of other nations. It must find markets, in the East, in Africa, anywhere; it must increase, by trade, the number of its serfs in Egypt, in India, on the Congo. But everywhere it finds competitors in other nations which rapidly enter into the same line of industrial development. And wars, continuous wars, must be fought for the supremacy in the world-market—wars for the possession of the East, wars for getting possession of the seas, wars for the right of imposing heavy duties on foreign merchandise. The thunder of European guns never ceases; whole generations are slaughtered from time to time; and we spend in armaments the third of the revenue of our States—a revenue raised, the poor know with what difficulties.

And finally, the injustice of our partition of wealth exercises the most deplorable effect on our morality. Our principles of morality say: "Love your neighbour as yourself"; but let a child follow this principle and take off his coat to give it to the shivering pauper, and his mother will tell him that he must never understand moral principles in their direct sense. If he lives according to them, he will go barefoot, without alleviating the misery around him! Morality is good on the lips, not in deeds. Our preachers say, "Who works, prays," and everyone endeavours to make others work for him. They say, "Never lie!", and politics are a big lie. And we accustom ourselves and our children to live under this double-faced morality, which is hypocrisy, and to conciliate our double-facedness by sophistry. Hypocrisy and sophistry become the very basis of our life. But society cannot live under such a morality. It cannot last so: it must, it will, be changed.

The question is thus no more a mere question of bread. It covers the whole field of human activity. But it has at its bottom a question of social economy, and we conclude: The means of production and of satisfaction of all needs of society, having been created by the common efforts of all, must be at the disposal of all. The private appropriation of requisites for production is neither just nor beneficial. All must be placed on the same footing as producers and consumers of wealth. That will be the only way for society to step out of the bad conditions which have been created by centuries of wars and oppression. That will be the only guarantee for further progress in a direction of equality and freedom, which have always been the real, although unspoken goal of humanity.

II

The views taken in the above as to the combination of efforts being the chief source of our wealth explain why most anarchists see in communism the only equitable solution as to the adequate remuneration of individual efforts. There was a time when a family engaged in agriculture supplemented by a few domestic trades could consider the corn they raised and the plain woolen cloth they wove as productions of their own and nobody else's labour. Even then such a view was not quite correct: there were forests cleared and roads built by common efforts; and even then the family had continually to apply for communal help, as is still the case in so many village communities. But now, in the extremely interwoven state of industry of which each branch supports all others, such an individualistic view can be held no more. If the iron trade and the cotton industry of this country have reached so high a degree of development, they have done so owing to the parallel growth of thousands of other industries, great and small; to the extension of the railway system; to an increase of knowledge among both the skilled engineers and the mass of the workmen; to a certain training in organisation slowly developed among producers; and, above all, to the world-trade which has itself grown up, thanks to works executed thousands of miles away. The Italians who died from cholera in digging the Suez Canal or from "tunnel-disease" in the St. Gothard Tunnel have contributed as much towards the enrichment of this country as the British girl who is prematurely growing old in serving a machine at Manchester; and this girl as much as the engineer who made a labour-saving improvement in our machinery. How can we pretend to estimate the exact part of each of them in the riches accumulated around us?

We may admire the inventive genius or the organising capacities of an iron lord; but we must recognise that all his genius and energy would not realise one-tenth of what they realise here if they were spent in dealing with Mongolian shepherds or Siberian peasants instead of British workmen, British engineers, and trustworthy managers. An English millionaire who succeeded in giving a powerful impulse to a branch of home industry was asked the other day what were, in his opinion, the real causes of his success? His answer was: "I always sought out the right man for a given branch of the concern, and I left him full independence—maintaining, of course, for myself the general supervision." "Did you never fail to find such men?" was the next question. "Never." "But in the new branches which you introduced you wanted a number of new inventions." "No doubt; we spent thousands in buying patents." This little colloquy sums up, in my opinion, the real case of those industrial undertakings which are quoted by the advocates of "an adequate remuneration of individual efforts" in the shape of millions bestowed on the managers of prosperous industries. It shows in how far the efforts are really "individual." Leaving aside the thousand conditions which sometimes permit a man to show, and sometimes prevent him from showing, his capacities to their full extent, it might be asked in how far the same capacities could bring out the same results, if the very same employer could find no trustworthy managers and no skilled workmen, and if hundreds of inventions were not stimulated by the mechanical turn of mind of so many inhabitants of this country.

The anarchists cannot consider, like the collectivists, that a remuneration which would be proportionate to the hours of labour spent by each person in the production of riches may be an ideal, or even an approach to an ideal, society. Without entering here into a discussion as to how far the exchange value of each merchandise is really measured now by the amount of labour necessary for its production—a separate study must be devoted to the subject—we must say that the collectivist ideal seems to us merely unrealisable in a society which has been brought to consider the necessaries for production as a common property. Such a society would be compelled to abandon the wage-system altogether. It appears impossible that the mitigated individualism of the collectivist school could co-exist with the partial communism implied by holding land and machinery in common—unless imposed by a powerful government, much more powerful than all those of our own times. The present wage-system has grown up from the appropriation of the necessaries for production by the few; it was a necessary condition for the growth of the present capitalist production; and it cannot outlive it, even if an attempt be made to pay to the worker the full value of his produce, and hours-of-labour-checks be substituted for money. Common possession of the necessaries for production implies the common enjoyment of the fruits of the common production; and we consider that an equitable organisation of society can only arise when every wage-system is abandoned, and when everybody, contributing for the common well-being to the full extent of his capacities, shall enjoy also from the common stock of society to the fullest possible extent of his needs.

We maintain, moreover, not only that communism is a desirable state of society, but that the growing tendency of modern society is precisely towards communism—free communism—notwithstanding the seemingly contradictory growth of individualism. In the growth of individualism (especially during the last three centuries) we see merely the endeavours of the individual towards emancipating himself from the steadily growing powers of capital and the State. But side by side with this growth we see also, throughout history up to our own times, the latent struggle of the producers of wealth to maintain the partial communism of old, as well as to reintroduce communist principles in a new shape, as soon as favourable conditions permit it. As soon as the communes of the tenth, eleventh, and twelfth centuries were enabled to start their own independent life, they gave a wide extension to work in common, to trade in common, and to a partial consumption in common. All this has disappeared. But the rural commune fights a hard struggle to maintain its old features, and it succeeds in maintaining them in many places of Eastern Europe, Switzerland, and even France and Germany; while new organisations, based on the same principles, never fail to grow up wherever it is possible.

Notwithstanding the egotistic turn given to the public mind by the merchant-production of our century, the communist tendency is continually reasserting itself and trying to make its way into public life. The penny bridge disappears before the public bridge; and the turnpike road before the free road. The same spirit pervades thousands of other institutions. Museums, free libraries, and free public schools; parks and pleasure grounds; paved and lighted streets, free for everybody's use; water supplied to private dwellings, with a growing tendency towards disregarding the exact amount of it used by the individual; tramways and railways which have already begun to introduce the season ticket or the uniform tax, and will surely go much further in this line when they are no longer private property: all these are tokens showing in what direction further progress is to be expected.

It is in the direction of putting the wants of the individual above the valuation of the services he has rendered, or might render, to society; in considering society as a whole, so intimately connected together that a service rendered to any individual is a service rendered to the whole society. The librarian of the British Museum does not ask the reader what have been his previous services to society; he simply gives him the books he requires; and for a uniform fee, a scientific society leaves its gardens and museums at the free disposal of each member. The crew of a lifeboat do not ask whether the men of a distressed ship are entitled to be rescued at a risk of life; and the Prisoners' Aid Society does not inquire what a released prisoner is worth. Here are men in need of a service; they are fellow men, and no further rights are required.

And if this very city, so egotistic today, be visited by a public calamity—let it be besieged, for example, like Paris in 1871, and experience during the siege a want of food—this very same city would be unanimous in proclaiming that the first needs to be satisfied are those of the children and old, no matter what services they may render or have rendered to society. And it would take care of the active defenders of the city, whatever the degrees of gallantry displayed by each of them. But, this tendency already existing, nobody will deny, I suppose, that, in proportion as humanity is relieved from its hard struggle for life, the same tendency will grow stronger. If our productive powers were fully applied to increasing the stock of the staple necessities for life; if a modification of the present conditions of property increased the number of producers by all those who are not producers of wealth now; and if manual labour reconquered its place of honour in society, the communist tendencies already existing would immediately enlarge their sphere of application.

Taking all this into account, and still more the practical aspects of the question as to how private property might become common property, most of the anarchists maintain that the very next step to be made by society, as soon as the present regime of property undergoes a modification, will be in a communist sense. We are communists. But our communism is not that of the authoritarian school: it is anarchist communism, communism without government, free communism. It is a synthesis of the two chief aims pursued by humanity since the dawn of its history — economic freedom and political freedom.

I have already said that anarchism means no-government. We know well that the word "anarchy" is also used in current phraseology as synonymous with disorder. But that meaning of "anarchy," being a derived one, implies at least two suppositions. It implies, first, that wherever there is no government there is disorder; and it implies, moreover, that order, due to a strong government and a strong police, is always beneficial. Both implications, however, are anything but proved. There is plenty of order — we should say, of harmony — in many branches of human activity where the government, happily, does not interfere. As to the beneficial effects of order, the kind of order that reigned at Naples under the Bourbons surely was not preferable to some disorder started by Garibaldi; while the Protestants of this country will probably say that the good deal of disorder made by Luther was preferable, at any rate, to the order which reigned under the Pope. While all agree that harmony is always desirable, there is no such unanimity about order, and still less about the "order" which is supposed to reign in our modern societies. So that we have no objection whatever to the use of the word "anarchy" as a negation of what has been often described as order.

By taking for our watchword "anarchy" in its sense of no-government, we intend to express a pronounced tendency of human society. In history we see that precisely those epochs when small parts of humanity broke down the power of their rulers and reassumed their freedom were epochs of the greatest progress, economic and intellectual. Be it the growth of the free cities, whose unrivalled monuments—free work of free associations of workers—still testify to the revival of mind and of the well-being of the citizen; be it the great movement which gave birth to the Reformation—those epochs when the individual recovered some part of his freedom witnessed the greatest progress. And if we carefully watch the present development of civilised nations, we cannot fail to discover in it a marked and ever-growing movement towards limiting more and more the sphere of action of government, so as to leave more and more liberty to the initiative of the individual. After having tried all kinds of government, and endeavoured to solve the insoluble problem of having a government "which might compel the individual to obedience, without escaping itself from obedience to collectivity," humanity is trying now to free itself from the bonds of any government whatever, and to respond to its needs of organisation by the free understanding between individuals pursuing the same common aims.

Home Rule, even for the smallest territorial unit or group, becomes a growing need. Free agreement is becoming a substitute for law. And free cooperation a substitute for governmental guardianship. One after the other those activities which were considered as the functions of government during the last two centuries are disputed; society moves better the less it is governed. And the more we study the advance made in this direction, as well as the inadequacy of governments to fulfill the expectations placed in them, the more we are bound to conclude that humanity, by steadily limiting the functions of government, is marching towards reducing them finally to nil. We already foresee a state of society where the liberty of the individual will be limited by no laws, no bonds—by nothing else but his own social habits and the necessity, which everyone feels, of finding cooperation, support, and sympathy among his neighbours.

Of course the no-government ethics will meet with at least as many objections as the no-capital economics. Our minds have been so nurtured in prejudices as to the providential functions of government that anarchist ideas must be received with distrust. Our whole education, from childhood to the grave, nurtures the belief in the necessity of a government and its beneficial effects. Systems of philosophy have been elaborated to support this view; history has been written from this standpoint; theories of law have been circulated and taught for the same purpose. All politics are based on the same principle, each politician saying to people he wants to support him: "Give me the governmental power; I will, I can, relieve you from the hardships of your present life." All our education is permeated with the same teachings. We may open any book of sociology, history, law, or ethics: everywhere we find government, its organisation, its deeds, playing so prominent a part that we grow accustomed to suppose that the State and the political men are everything; that there is nothing behind the big statesmen. The same teachings are daily repeated in the Press. Whole columns are filled up with minutest records of parliamentary debates, of movements of political persons. And, while reading these columns, we too often forget that besides those few men whose importance has been so swollen up as to overshadow humanity, there is an immense body of men—mankind, in fact—growing and dying, living in happiness or sorrow, labouring and consuming, thinking and creating.

And yet, if we revert from the printed matter to our real life, and cast a broad glance on society as it is, we are struck with the infinitesimal part played by government in our life. Millions of human beings live and die without having had anything to do with government. Every day millions of transactions are made without the slightest interference of government; and those who enter into agreements have not the slightest intention of breaking bargains. Nay, those agreements which are not protected by government (those of the exchange, or card debts) are perhaps better kept than any others. The simple habit of keeping one's word, the desire of not losing confidence, are quite sufficient in an overwhelming majority of cases to enforce the keeping of agreements. Of course it may be said that there is still the government which might enforce them if necessary. But without speaking of the numberless cases which could not even be brought before a court, everyone who has the slightest acquaintance with trade will undoubtedly confirm the assertion that, if there were not so strong a feeling of honour in keeping agreements, trade itself would become utterly impossible. Even those merchants and manufacturers who feel not the slightest remorse when poisoning their customers with all kinds of abominable drugs, duly labeled, even they also keep their commercial agreements. But if such a relative morality as commercial honesty exists now under the present conditions, when enrichment is the chief motive, the same feeling will further develop very quickly as soon as robbing someone of the fruits of his labour is no longer the economic basis of our life.

Another striking feature of our century tells in favour of the same no-government tendency. It is the steady enlargement of the field covered by private initiative, and the recent growth of large organisations resulting merely and simply from free agreement. The railway net of Europe—a confederation of so many scores of separate societies—and the direct transport of passengers and merchandise over so many lines which were built independently and federated together, without even so much as a Central Board of European Railways, is a most striking instance of what is already done by mere agreement. If fifty years ago somebody had predicted that railways built by so many separate companies finally would constitute so perfect a net as they do today, he surely would have been treated as a fool. It would have been urged that so many companies, prosecuting their own interests, would never agree without an International Board of Railways, supported by an International Convention of the European States, and endowed with governmental powers. But no such board was resorted to, and the agreement came nevertheless. The Dutch associations of ship and boat owners are now extending their organisations over the rivers of Germany and even to the shipping trade of the Baltic. The numberless amalgamated manufacturers' associations, and the syndicates of France, are so many instances in point. If it be argued that many of these organisations are organisations for exploitation, that proves nothing, because, if men pursuing their own egotistic, often very narrow, interests can agree together, better inspired men, compelled to be more closely connected with other groups, will necessarily agree still more easily and still better.

But there also is no lack of free organisations for nobler pursuits. One of the noblest achievements of our century is undoubtedly the Lifeboat Association. Since its first humble start, it has saved no less than thirty-two thousand human lives. It makes appeal to the noblest instincts of man; its activity is entirely dependent upon devotion to the common cause, while its internal organisation is entirely based upon the independence of the local committees. The Hospitals

Association and hundreds of like organisations, operating on a large scale and covering each a wide field, may also be mentioned under this head. But, while we know everything about governments and their deeds, what do we know about the results achieved by free cooperation? Thousands of volumes have been written to record the acts of governments; the most trifling amelioration due to law has been recorded; its good effects have been exaggerated, its bad effects passed by in silence. But where is the book recording what has been achieved by free cooperation of well-inspired men? At the same time, hundreds of societies are constituted every day for the satisfaction of some of the infinitely varied needs of civilised man. We have societies for all possible kinds of studies — some of them embracing the whole field of natural science, others limited to a small special branch; societies for gymnastics, for shorthand-writing, for the study of a separate author, for games and all kinds of sports, for forwarding the science of maintaining life, and for favouring the art of destroying it; philosophical and industrial, artistic and anti-artistic; for serious work and for mere amusement — in short, there is not a single direction in which men exercise their faculties without combining together for the accomplishment of some common aim. Every day new societies are formed, while every year the old ones aggregate together into larger units, federate across the national frontiers, and cooperate in some common work.

The most striking feature of these numberless free growths is that they continually encroach on what was formerly the domain of the State or the Municipality. A householder in a Swiss village on the banks of Lake Leman belongs now to at least a dozen different societies which supply him with what is considered elsewhere as a function of the municipal government. Free federation of independent communes for temporary or permanent purposes lies at the very bottom of Swiss life, and to these federations many a part of Switzerland is indebted for its roads and fountains, its rich vineyards, well-kept forests, and meadows which the foreigner admires. And besides these small societies, substituting themselves for the State within some limited sphere, do we not see other societies doing the same on a much wider scale?

One of the most remarkable societies which has recently arisen is undoubtedly the Red Cross Society. To slaughter men on the battle-fields, that remains the duty of the State; but these very States recognise their inability to take care of their own wounded: they abandon the task, to a great extent, to private initiative. What a deluge of mockeries would not have been cast over the poor "Utopist" who should have dared to say twenty-five years ago that the care of the wounded might be left to private societies! "Nobody would go into the dangerous places! Hospitals would all gather where there was no need of them! National rivalries would result in the poor soldiers dying without any help, and so on" — such would have been the outcry. The war of 1871 has shown how perspicacious those prophets are who never believe in human intelligence, devotion, and good sense.

These facts — so numerous and so customary that we pass by without even noticing them — are in our opinion one of the most prominent features of the second half of the nineteenth century. The just-mentioned organisms grew up so naturally, they so rapidly extended and so easily aggregated together, they are such unavoidable outgrowths of the multiplication of needs of the civilised man, and they so well replace State-interference, that we must recognise in them a growing factor of our life. Modern progress is really towards the free aggregation of free individuals so as to supplant government in all those functions which formerly were entrusted to it, and which it mostly performed so badly.

As to parliamentary rule and representative government altogether, they are rapidly falling into decay. The few philosophers who already have shown their defects have only timidly summed up the growing public discontent. It is becoming evident that it is merely stupid to elect a few men and to entrust them with the task of making laws on all possible subjects, of which subjects most of them are utterly ignorant. It is becoming understood that majority rule is as defective as any other kind of rule; and humanity searches and finds new channels for resolving the pending questions The Postal Union did not elect an international postal parliament in order to make laws for all postal organisations adherent to the Union. The railways of Europe did not elect an international railway parliament in order to regulate the running of the trains and the partition of the income of international traffic. And the Meteorological and Geological Societies of Europe did not elect either meteorological or geological parliaments to plan polar stations, or to establish a uniform subdivision of geological formations and a uniform coloration of geological maps. They proceeded by means of agreement. To agree together they resorted to congresses; but, while sending delegates to their congresses they did not say to them, "Vote about everything you like—we shall obey." They put forward questions and discussed them first themselves; then they sent delegates acquainted with the special question to be discussed at the congress, and they sent delegates—not rulers. Their delegates returned from the congress with no laws in their pockets, but with proposals of agreements. Such is the way assumed now (the very old way, too) for dealing with questions of public interest—not the way of law-making by means of a representative government.

Representative government has accomplished its historical mission; it has given a mortal blow to court-rule; and by its debates it has awakened public interest in public questions. But to see in it the government of the future socialist society is to commit a gross error. Each economic phase of life implies its own political phase; and it is impossible to touch the very basis of the present economic life—private property—without a corresponding change in the very basis of the political organisation. Life already shows in which direction the change will be made. Not in increasing the powers of the State, but in resorting to free organisation and free federation in all those branches which are now considered as attributes of the State.

The objections to the above may be easily foreseen. It will be said of course: "But what is to be done with those who do not keep their agreements? What with those who are not inclined to work? What with those who would prefer breaking the written laws of society, or—on the anarchist hypothesis—its unwritten customs? Anarchism may be good for a higher humanity—not for the men of our own times."

First of all, there are two kinds of agreements: there is the free one which is entered upon by free consent, as a free choice between different courses equally open to each of the agreeing parties. And there is the enforced agreement, imposed by one party upon the other, and accepted by the latter from sheer necessity; in fact, it is no agreement at all; it is a mere submission to necessity. Unhappily, the great bulk of what are now described as "agreements" belong to the latter category. When a workman sells his labour to an employer and knows perfectly well that some part of the value of his produce will be unjustly taken by the employer; when he sells it without even the slightest guarantee of being employed so much as six consecutive months, it is a sad mockery to call that a free contract. Modern economists may call it free, but the father of political economy — Adam Smith — was never guilty of such a misrepresentation. As long as three-quarters of humanity are compelled to enter into agreements of that description, force is of course necessary, both to enforce the supposed agreements and to maintain such a state of things. Force — and a great deal of force — is necessary to prevent the labourers from taking possession of what they consider unjustly appropriated by the few; and force is necessary to continually bring new "uncivilised nations" under the same conditions.

But we do not see the necessity of force for enforcing agreements freely entered upon. We never heard of a penalty imposed on a man who belonged to the crew of a lifeboat and at a given moment preferred to abandon the association. All that his comrades would do with him, if he were guilty of a gross neglect, would probably be to refuse to have anything further to do with him. Nor did we hear of fines imposed on a contributor to the dictionary for a delay in his work, or of gendarmes driving the volunteers of Garibaldi to the battlefield. Free agreements need not be enforced.

As to the so-often repeated objection that no one would labour if he were not compelled to do so by sheer necessity, we heard enough of it before the emancipation of slaves in America, as well as before the emancipation of serfs in Russia. And we have had the opportunity of appreciating it at its just value. So we shall not try to convince those who can be convinced only by accomplished facts. As to those who reason, they ought to know that, if it really was so with some parts of humanity at its lowest stages, or if it is so with some small communities, or separate individuals, brought to sheer despair by ill success in their struggle against unfavourable conditions, it is not so with the bulk of the civilised nations. With us, work is a habit, and idleness an artificial growth. Of course, when to be a manual worker means to be compelled to work all one's life long for ten hours a day, and often more, at producing some part of something — a pin's head, for instance; when it means to be paid wages on which a family can live only on the condition of the strictest limitation of all its needs; when it means to be always under the menace of being thrown tomorrow out of employment — and we know how frequent are the industrial crises, and what misery they imply; when it means, in a very great number of cases, premature death in a paupers' infirmary, if not in the workhouse; when to be a manual worker signifies to wear a life-long stamp of inferiority in the eyes of those very people who live on the work of these "hands;" when it always means the renunciation of all those higher enjoyments that science and art give to man—oh, then there is no wonder that everybody—the manual workers as well—has but one dream: that of rising to a condition where others would work for him.

Overwork is repulsive to human nature—not work. Overwork for supplying the few with luxury—not work for the well-being of all. Work is a physiological necessity, a necessity of spending accumulated bodily energy, a necessity which is health and life itself. If so many branches of useful work are so reluctantly done now, it is merely because they mean overwork, or they are improperly organised. But we know—old Franklin knew it—that four hours of useful work every day would be more than sufficient for supplying everybody with the comfort of a moderately well-to-do middle-class house, if we all gave ourselves to productive work, and if we did not waste our productive powers as we do waste them now.

As to the childish question, repeated for fifty years: "Who would do disagreeable work?" frankly I regret that none of our savants has ever been brought to do it, be it for only one day in his life. If there is still work which is really disagreeable in itself, it is only because our scientific men have never cared to consider the means of rendering it less so. They have always known that there were plenty of starving men who would do it for a few cents a day.

As to the third—the chief—objection, which maintains the necessity of a government for punishing those who break the law of society, there is so much to say about it that it hardly can be touched incidentally. The more we study the question, the more we are brought to the conclusion that society itself is responsible for the anti-social deeds perpetrated in its midst, and that no punishment, no prisons, and no hangmen can diminish the numbers of such deeds; nothing short of a reorganisation of society itself.

Three quarters of all the acts which are brought before our courts every year have their origin, either directly or indirectly, in the present disorganised state of society with regard to the production and distribution of wealth—not in perversity of human nature. As to the relatively few anti-social deeds which result from anti-social inclinations of separate individuals, it is not by prisons, nor even by resorting to the hangmen, that we can diminish their numbers. By our prisons, we merely multiply them and render them worse. By our detectives, our "price of blood," our executions, and our jails, we spread in society such a terrible flow of basest passions and habits, that he who should realise the effects of these institutions to their full extent would be frightened by what society is doing under the pretext of maintaining morality. We must search for other remedies, and the remedies have been indicated long since.

Of course now, when a mother in search of food and shelter for her children must pass by shops filled with the most refined delicacies of refined gluttony; when gorgeous and insolent luxury is displayed side by side with the most execrable misery; when the dog and the horse of a rich man are far better cared for than millions of children whose mothers earn a pitiful salary in the pit or the manufactory; when each "modest" evening dress of a lady represents eight months, or one year, of human labour; when enrichment at somebody else's expense is the avowed aim of the "upper classes," and no distinct boundary can be traced between honest and dishonest means of making money—then force is the only means for maintaining such a state of things. Then an army of policemen, judges, and hangmen becomes a necessary institution

But if all our children—all children are our children—received a sound instruction and education—and we have the means of giving it; if every family lived in a decent home—and they could at the present high pitch of our production; if every boy and girl were taught a handicraft at the same time as he or she receives scientific instruction, and not to be a manual producer of wealth were considered as a token of inferiority; if men lived in closer contact with one another, and had continually to come into contact on those public affairs which now are vested in the few; and if, in consequence of a closer contact, we were brought to take as lively an interest in our neighbours' difficulties and pains as we formerly took in those of our kinsfolk—then we should not resort to policemen and judges, to prisons and executions. Anti-social deeds would be nipped in the bud, not punished. The few contests which would arise would be easily settled by arbitrators; and no more force would be necessary to impose their decisions than is required now for enforcing the decisions of the family tribunals of China.

And here we are brought to consider a great question: what would become of morality in a society which recognised no laws and proclaimed the full freedom of the individual? Our answer is plain.

Public morality is independent from, and anterior to, law and religion. Until now, the teachings of morality have been associated with religious teachings. But the influence which religious teachings formerly exercised on the mind has faded of late, and the sanction which morality derived from religion has no longer the power it formerly had. Millions and millions grow in our cities who have lost the old faith. Is it a reason for throwing morality overboard, and for treating it with the same sarcasm as primitive cosmogony?

Obviously not. No society is possible without certain principles of morality generally recognised. If everyone grew accustomed to deceiving his fellow-men; if we never could rely on each other's promise and words; if everyone treated his fellow as an enemy, against whom every means of warfare is justifiable—no society could exist. And we see, in fact, that notwithstanding the decay of religious beliefs, the principles of morality remain unshaken. We even see irreligious people trying to raise the current standard of morality. The fact is that moral principles are independent of religious beliefs: they are anterior to them. The primitive Tchuktchis have no religion: they have only superstitions and fear of the hostile forces of nature; and nevertheless we find with them the very same principles of morality which are taught by Christians and Buddhists, Mussulmans and Hebrews. Nay, some of their practises imply a much higher standard of tribal morality than that which appears in our civilised society.

In fact, each new religion takes its moral principles from the only real stock of morality—the moral habits which grow with men as soon as they unite to live together in tribes, cities, or nations. No animal society is possible without resulting in a growth of certain moral habits of mutual support and even self-sacrifice for the common well-being. These habits are a necessary condition for the welfare of the species in its struggle for life—cooperation of individuals being a much more important factor in the struggle for the preservation of the species than the so-much-spoken-of physical struggle between individuals for the means of existence. The "fittest" in the organic world are those who grow accustomed to life in society; and life in society necessarily implies moral habits. As to mankind, it has during its long existence developed in its midst a nucleus of social habits, of moral habits, which cannot disappear as long as human societies exist. And therefore, notwithstanding the influences to the contrary which are now at work in consequence of our present economic relations, the nucleus of our moral habits continues to exist.

Law and religion only formulate them and endeavour to enforce them by their sanction.

Whatever the variety of theories of morality, all can be brought under three chief categories: the morality of religion; the utilitarian morality; and the theory of moral habits resulting from the very needs of life in society. Each religious morality sanctifies its prescriptions by making them originate from revelation; and it tries to impress its teachings on the mind by a promise of reward, or punishment, either in this or in a future life. The utilitarian morality maintains the idea of reward, but it finds it in man himself. It invites men to analyse their pleasures, to classify them, and to give preference to those which are most intense and most durable. We must recognise, however, that, although it has exercised some influence, this system has been judged too artificial by the great mass of human beings. And finally—whatever its varieties—there is the third system of morality which sees in moral actions—in those actions which are most powerful in rendering men best fitted for life in society—a mere necessity of the individual to enjoy the joys of his brethren, to suffer when some of his brethren are suffering; a habit and a second nature, slowly elaborated and perfected by life in society. That is the morality of mankind; and that is also the morality of anarchism.

Such are, in a very brief summary, the leading principles of anarchism. Each of them hurts many a prejudice, and yet each of them results from an analysis of the very tendencies displayed by human society. Each of them is rich in consequences and implies a thorough revision of many a current opinion. And anarchism is not a mere insight into a remote future. Already now, whatever the sphere of action of the individual, he can act, either in accordance with anarchist principles or on an opposite line. And all that may be done in that direction will be done in the direction to which further development goes. All that may be done in the opposite way will be an attempt to force humanity to go where it will not go.

Anarchist Morality

1897

(Editor's Note: In this pamphlet, Kropotkin discusses the possibility of basing societies on ethical and moral considerations rather than on coercive laws.)

I

The history of human thought recalls the swinging of a pendulum which takes centuries to swing. After a long period of slumber comes a moment of awakening. Then thought frees herself from the chains with which those interested — rulers, lawyers, clerics — have carefully enwound her.

She shatters the chains. She subjects to severe criticism all that has been taught her, and lays bare the emptiness of the religious, political, legal, and social prejudices amid which she has vegetated. She starts research in new paths, enriches our knowledge with new discoveries, creates new sciences.

But the inveterate enemies of thought — the government, the lawgiver, and the priest — soon recover from their defeat. By degrees they gather together their scattered forces, and remodel their faith and their code of laws to adapt them to the new needs. Then, profiting by the servility of thought and of character, which they themselves have so effectually cultivated; profiting, too, by the momentary disorganization of society, taking advantage of the laziness of some, the greed of others, the best hopes of many, they softly creep back to their work by first of all taking possession of childhood through education.

A child's spirit is weak. It is so easy to coerce it by fear. This they do. They make the child timid, and then they talk to him of the torments of hell. They conjure up before him the sufferings of the condemned, the vengeance of an implacable god. The next minute they will be chattering of the horrors of revolution, and using some excess of the revolutionists to make the child "a friend of order." The priest accustoms the child to the idea of law, to make it obey better what he calls the "divine law," and the lawyer prates of divine law, that the civil law may be the better obeyed.

And by that habit of submission, with which we are only too familiar, the thought of the next generation retains this religious twist, which is at once servile and authoritative, for authority and servility walk ever hand in hand.

During these slumbrous interludes, morals are rarely discussed. Religious practices and judicial hypocrisy take their place. People do not criticize, they let themselves be drawn by habit, or indifference. They do not put themselves out for or against the established morality. They do their best to make their actions appear to accord with their professions.

All that was good, great, generous or independent in man, little by little becomes moss-grown; rusts like a disused knife. A lie becomes a virtue, a platitude a duty. To enrich oneself, to seize one's opportunities, to exhaust one's intelligence, zeal and energy, no matter how, become the watchwords of the comfortable classes, as well as of the crowd of poor folk whose ideal is to appear bourgeois. Then the degradation of the ruler and of the judge, of the clergy and of the more or less comfortable classes becomes so revolting that the pendulum begins to swing the other way.

Little by little, youth frees itself. It flings overboard its prejudices, and it begins to criticize. Thought reawakens, at first among the few; but insensibly the awakening reaches the majority. The impulse is given, the revolution follows.

And each time the question of morality comes up again. "Why should I follow the principles of this hypocritical morality?" asks the brain, released from religious terrors. "Why should any morality be obligatory?"

Then people try to account for the moral sentiment that they meet at every turn without having explained it to themselves. And they will never explain it so long as they believe it a privilege of human nature, so long as they do not descend to animals, plants and rocks to understand it. They seek the answer, however, in the science of the hour.

And, if we may venture to say so, the more the basis of conventional morality, or rather of the hypocrisy that fills its place is sapped, the more the moral plane of society is raised. It is above all at such times precisely when folks are criticizing and denying it, that moral sentiment makes the most progress. It is then that it grows, that it is raised and refined.

Years ago the youth of Russia were passionately agitated by this very question. "I will be immoral!" a young nihilist came and said to his friend, thus translating into action the thoughts that gave him no rest. "I will be immoral, and why should I not? Because the Bible wills it? But the Bible is only a collection of Babylonian and Hebrew traditions, traditions collected and put together like the Homeric poems, or as is being done still with Basque poems and Mongolian legends. Must I then go back to the state of mind of the half-civilized peoples of the East?"

"Must I be moral because Kant tells me of a categoric imperative, of a mysterious command which comes to me from the depths of my own being and bids me be moral? But why should this 'categoric imperative' exercise a greater authority over my actions than that other imperative, which at times may command me to get drunk. A word, nothing but a word, like the words 'Providence,' or 'Destiny,' invented to conceal our ignorance."

"Or perhaps I am to be moral to oblige Bentham, who wants me to believe that I shall be happier if I drown to save a passerby who has fallen into the river than if I watched him drown?"

"Or perhaps because such has been my education? Because my mother taught me morality? Shall I then go and kneel down in a church, honor the Queen, bow before the judge I know for a scoundrel, simply because our mothers, our good ignorant mothers, have taught us such a pack of nonsense?"

"I am prejudiced—like everyone else. I will try to rid myself of prejudice! Even though immorality be distasteful, I will yet force myself to be immoral, as when I was a boy I forced myself to give up fearing the dark, the churchyard, ghosts and dead people—all of which I had been taught to fear."

"It will be immoral to snap a weapon abused by religion; I will do it, were it only to protect against the hypocrisy imposed on us in the name of a word to which the name morality has been given!"

Such was the way in which the youth of Russia reasoned when they broke with old-world prejudices, and unfurled this banner of nihilist or rather of anarchist philosophy: to bend the knee to no authority whatsoever, however respected; to accept no principle so long as it is unestablished by reason.

Need we add, that after pitching into the wastepaper basket the teachings of their fathers, and burning all systems of morality, the nihilist youth developed in their midst a nucleus of moral customs, infinitely superior to anything that their fathers had practiced under the control of the "Gospel," of the "Conscience," of the "Categoric Imperative," or of the "Recognized Advantage" of the utilitarian. But before answering the question, "Why am I to be moral?" let us see if the question is well put; let us analyze the motives of human action.

II

When our ancestors wished to account for what led men to act in one way or another, they did so in a very simple fashion. Down to the present day, certain catholic images may be seen that represent this explanation. A man is going on his way, and without being in the least aware of it, carries a devil on his left shoulder and an angel on his right. The devil prompts him to do evil, the angel tries to keep him back. And if the angel gets the best of it and the man remains virtuous, three other angels catch him up and carry him to heaven. In this way everything is explained wondrously well.

Old Russian nurses full of such lore will tell you never to put a child to bed without unbuttoning the collar of its shirt. A warm spot at the bottom of the neck should be left bare, where the guardian angel may nestle. Otherwise the devil will worry the child even in its sleep.

These artless conceptions are passing away. But though the old words disappear, the essential idea remains the same.

Well brought up folks no longer believe in the devil, but as their ideas are no more rational than those of our nurses, they do but disguise devil and angel under a pedantic wordiness honored with the name of philosophy. They do not say "devil" nowadays, but "the flesh," or "the passions." The "angel" is replaced by the words "conscience" or "soul," by "reflection of the thought of a divine creator" or "the Great Architect," as the Freemasons say. But man's action is still represented as the result of a struggle between two hostile elements. And a man is always considered virtuous just in the degree to which one of these two elements — the soul or conscience — is victorious over the other — the flesh or passions.

It is easy to understand the astonishment of our great-grandfathers when the English philosophers, and later the Encyclopedists, began to affirm in opposition to these primitive ideas that the devil and the angel had nothing to do with human action, but that all acts of man, good or bad, useful or baneful, arise from a single motive: the lust for pleasure.

The whole religious confraternity, and, above all, the numerous sects of the pharisees shouted "immorality." They covered the thinkers with insult, they excommunicated them. And when later on in the course of the century the same ideas were again taken up by Bentham, John Stuart Mill, Tchernischevsky, and a host of others, and when these thinkers began to affirm and prove that egoism, or the lust for pleasure, is the true motive of all our actions, the maledictions redoubled. The books were banned by a conspiracy of silence; the authors were treated as dunces.

And yet what can be more true than the assertion they made?

Here is a man who snatches its last mouthful of bread from a child. Every one agrees in saying that he is a horrible egoist, that he is guided solely by self-love.

But now here is another man, whom every one agrees to recognize as virtuous. He shares his last bit of bread with the hungry, and strips off his coat to clothe the naked. And the moralists, sticking to their religious jargon, hasten to say that this man carries the love of his neighbor to the point of self-abnegation, that he obeys a wholly different passion from that of the egoist. And yet with a little reflection we soon discover that however great the difference between the two actions in their result for humanity, the motive has still been the same. It is the quest of pleasure.

If the man who gives away his last shirt found no pleasure in doing so, he would not do it. If he found pleasure in taking bread from a child, he would do that but this is distasteful to him. He finds pleasure in giving, and so he gives. If it were not inconvenient to cause confusion by employing in a new sense words that have a recognized meaning, it might be said that in both cases the men acted under the impulse of their egoism. Some have actually said this, to give prominence to the thought and precision to the idea by presenting it in a form that strikes the imagination, and at the same time to destroy the myth which asserts that these two acts have two different motives. They have the same motive, the quest of pleasure, or the avoidance of pain, which comes to the same thing.

Take for example the worst of scoundrels: a Thiers, who massacres thirty-five thousand Parisians, or an assassin who butchers a whole family in order that he may wallow in debauchery. They do it because for the moment the desire of glory or of money gains in their minds the upper hand of every other desire. Even pity and compassion are extinguished for the moment by this other desire, this other thirst. They act almost automatically to satisfy a craving of their nature. Or again, putting aside the stronger passions, take the petty man who deceives his friends, who lies at every step to get out of somebody the price of a pot of beer, or from sheer love of brag, or from cunning. Take the employer who cheats his workmen to buy jewels for his wife or his mistress. Take any petty scoundrel you like. He again only obeys an impulse. He seeks the satisfaction of a craving, or he seeks to escape what would give him trouble.

We are almost ashamed to compare such petty scoundrels to the martyr who fights to free the oppressed, and like a Russian nihilist mounts the scaffold. So vastly different for humanity are the results of these two lives; so much do we feel ourselves drawn towards the one and repelled by the other.

And yet were you to talk to such a martyr, to the woman who is about to be hanged, even just as she nears the gallows, she would tell you that she would not exchange either her life or her death for the life of the petty scoundrel who lives on the money stolen from his work-people. In her life, in the struggle against monstrous might, she finds her highest joys. Everything else outside the struggle, all the little joys of the bourgeois and his little troubles seem to her so contemptible, so tiresome, so pitiable! "You do not live, you vegetate," she would reply; "I have lived."

We are speaking of course of the deliberate, conscious acts of men, reserving for the present what we have to say about that immense series of unconscious, all but mechanical acts, which occupy so large a portion of our life. In his deliberate, conscious acts man always seeks what will give him pleasure.

One man gets drunk, and every day lowers himself to the condition of a brute because he seeks in liquor the nervous excitement that he cannot obtain from his own nervous system. Another does not get drunk; he takes no liquor, even though he finds it pleasant, because he wants to keep the freshness of his thoughts and the plentitude of his powers, that he may be able to taste other pleasures which he prefers to drink. But how does he act if not like the judge of good living who, after glancing at the menu of an elaborate dinner rejects one dish that he likes very well to eat his fill of another that he likes better.

When a woman deprives herself of her last piece of bread to give it to the first comer, when she takes off her own scanty rags to cover another woman who is cold, while she herself shivers on the deck of a vessel, she does so because she would suffer infinitely more in seeing a hungry man, or a woman starved with cold, than in shivering or feeling hungry herself. She escapes a pain of which only those who have felt it know the intensity.

When the Australian, quoted by Guyau, wasted away beneath the idea that he has not yet revenged his kinsman's death; when he grows thin and pale, a prey to the consciousness of his cowardice, and does not return to life till he has done the deed of vengeance, he performs this action, a heroic one sometimes, to free himself of a feeling which possesses him, to regain that inward peace which is the highest of pleasures.

When a troupe of monkeys has seen one of its members fall in consequence of a hunter's shot, and comes to besiege his tent and claim the body despite the threatening gun; when at length the Elder of the band goes right in, first threatens the hunter, then implores him, and finally by his lamentations induces him to give up the corpse, which the groaning troupe carry off into the forest, these monkeys obey a feeling of compassion stronger than all considerations of personal security. This feeling in them exceeds all others. Life itself loses its attraction for them while they are not sure whether they can restore life to their comrade or not. This feeling becomes so oppressive that the poor brutes do everything to get rid of it.

When the ants rush by thousands into the flames of the burning ant-hill, which that evil beast, man, has set on fire, and perish by hundreds to rescue their larvae, they again obey a craving to save their offspring. They risk everything for the sake of bringing away the larvae that they have brought up with more care than many women bestow on their children.

To seek pleasure, to avoid pain, is the general line of action (some would say law) of the organic world.

Without this quest of the agreeable, life itself would be impossible. Organisms would disintegrate, life cease.

Thus whatever a man's actions and line of conduct may be, he does what he does in obedience to a craving of his nature. The most repulsive actions, no less than actions which are indifferent or most attractive, are all equally dictated by a need of the individual who performs them. Let him act as he may, the individual acts as he does because he finds a pleasure in it, or avoids, or thinks he avoids, a pain.

Here we have a well-established fact. Here we have the essence of what has been called the egoistic theory.

Very well, are we any better off for having reached this general conclusion?

Yes, certainly we are. We have conquered a truth and destroyed a prejudice which lies at the root of all prejudices. All materialist philosophy in its relation to man is implied in this conclusion. But does it follow that all the actions of the individual are indifferent, as some have hastened to conclude? This is what we have now to see.

III

We have seen that men's actions (their deliberate and conscious actions, for we will speak afterwards of unconscious habits) all have the same origin. Those that are called virtuous and those that are designated as vicious, great devotions and petty knaveries, acts that attract and acts that repel, all spring from a common source. All are performed in answer to some need of the individual's nature. All have for their end the quest of pleasure, the desire to avoid pain.

We have seen this in the last section, which is but a very succinct summary of a mass of facts that might be brought forward in support of this view.

It is easy to understand how this explanation makes those still imbued with religious principles cry out. It leaves no room for the supernatural. It throws over the idea of an immortal soul. If man only acts in obedience to the needs of his nature, if he is, so to say, but a "conscious automaton," what becomes of the immortal soul? What of immortality, that last refuge of those who have known too few pleasures and too many sufferings, and who dream of finding some compensation in another world?

It is easy to understand how people who have grown up in prejudice and with but little confidence in science, which has so often deceived them, people who are led by feeling rather than thought, reject an explanation which takes from them their last hope.

IV

Mosaic, Buddhist, Christian and Mussulman theologians have had recourse to divine inspiration to distinguish between good and evil. They have seen that man, be he savage or civilized, ignorant or learned, perverse or kindly and honest, always knows if he is acting well or ill, especially always knows if he is acting ill. And as they have found no explanation of this general fact, they have put it down to divine inspiration. Metaphysical philosophers, on their side, have told us of conscience, of a mystic "imperative," and, after all, have changed nothing but the phrases.

But neither have known how to estimate the very simple and very striking fact that animals living in societies are also able to distinguish between good and evil, just as man does. Moreover, their conceptions of good and evil are of the same nature as those of man. Among the best developed representatives of each separate class—fish, insects, birds, mammals—they are even identical.

Forel, that inimitable observer of ants, has shown by a mass of observations and facts that when an ant who has her crop well filled with honey meets other ants with empty stomachs, the latter immediately ask her for food. And amongst these little insects it is the duty of the satisfied ant to disgorge the honey that her hungry friends may also be satisfied. Ask the ants if it would be right to refuse food to other ants of the same anthill when one has had one's share. They will answer, by actions impossible to mistake, that it would be extremely wrong. So selfish an ant would be more harshly treated than enemies of another species. If such a thing happens during a battle between two different species, the ants would stop fighting to fall upon their selfish comrade. This fact has been proved by experiments which exclude all doubt.

Or again, ask the sparrows living in your garden if it is right not to give notice to all the little society when some crumbs are thrown out, so that all may come and share in the meal. Ask them if that hedge sparrow has done right in stealing from his neighbor's nest those straws he had picked up, straws which the thief was too lazy to go and collect himself. The sparrows will answer that he is very wrong, by flying at the robber and pecking him.

Or ask the marmots if it is right for one to refuse access to his underground storehouse to other marmots of the same colony. They will answer that it is very wrong, by quarrelling in all sorts of ways with the miser.

Finally, ask primitive man if it is right to take food in the tent of a member of the tribe during his absence. He will answer that, if the man could get his food for himself, it was very wrong. On the other hand, if he was weary or in want, he ought to take food where he finds it; but in such a case, he will do well to leave his cap or his knife, or even a bit of knotted string, so that the absent hunter may know on his return that a friend has been there, not a robber. Such a precaution will save him the anxiety caused by the possible presence of a marauder near his tent.

Thousands of similar facts might be quoted, whole books might be written, to show how identical are the conceptions of good and evil amongst men and the other animals.

The ant, the bird, the marmot, the savage have read neither Kant nor the fathers of the Church nor even Moses. And yet all have the same idea of good and evil. And if you reflect for a moment on what lies at the bottom of this idea, you will see directly that what is considered good among ants, marmots, and Christian or atheist moralists is that which is useful for the preservation of the race; and that which is considered evil is that which is hurtful for race preservation. Not for the individual, as Bentham and Mill put it, but fair and good for the whole race.

The idea of good and evil has thus nothing to do with religion or a mystic conscience. It is a natural need of animal races. And when founders of religions, philosophers, and moralists tell us of divine or metaphysical entities, they are only recasting what each ant, each sparrow practices in its little society.

Is this useful to society? Then it is good. Is this hurtful? Then it is bad.

This idea may be extremely restricted among inferior animals, it may be enlarged among the more advanced animals; but its essence always remains the same.

Among ants it does not extend beyond the anthill. All sociable customs, all rules of good behavior are applicable only to the individuals in that one anthill, not to any others. One anthill will not consider another as belonging to the same family, unless under some exceptional circumstances, such as a common distress falling upon both. In the same way the sparrows in the Luxembourg Gardens in Paris, though they will mutually aid one another in a striking manner, will fight to the death with another sparrow from the Monge Square who may dare to venture into the Luxembourg. And the savage will look upon a savage of another tribe as a person to whom the usages of his own tribe do not apply. It is even allowable to sell to him, and to sell is always to rob the buyer more or less; buyer or seller, one or other is always "sold." A Tchoutche would think it a crime to sell to the members of his tribe: to them he gives without any reckoning. And civilized man, when at last he understands the relations between himself and others. In the simplest Papuan, close relations, though imperceptible at the first glance, will extend his principles of solidarity to the whole human race, and even to the animals. The idea enlarges, but its foundation remains the same.

On the other hand, the conception of good or evil varies according to the degree of intelligence or of knowledge acquired. There is nothing unchangeable about it.

Primitive man may have thought it very right—that is, useful to the race—to eat his aged parents when they became a charge upon the community—a very heavy charge in the main. He may have also thought it useful to the community to kill his new-born children, and only keep two or three in each family, so that the mother could suckle them until they were three years old and lavish more of her tenderness upon them.

In our days ideas have changed, but the means of subsistence are no longer what they were in the Stone Age. Civilized man is not in the position of the savage family who have to choose between two evils: either to eat the aged parents or else all to get insufficient nourishment and soon find themselves unable to feed both the aged parents and the young children. We must transport ourselves into those ages, which we can scarcely call up in our mind, before we can understand that in the circumstances then existing, half-savage man may have reasoned rightly enough.

Ways of thinking may change. The estimate of what is useful or hurtful to the race changes, but the foundation remains the same. And if we wished to sum up the whole philosophy of the animal kingdom in a single phrase, we should see that ants, birds, marmots, and men are agreed on one point.

The morality which emerges from the observation of the whole animal kingdom may be summed up in the words: "Do to others what you would have them do to you in the same circumstances."

And it adds: "Take note that this is merely a piece of advice; but this advice is the fruit of the long experience of animals in society. And among the great mass of social animals, man included, it has become habitual to act on this principle. Indeed without this no society could exist, no race could have vanquished the natural obstacles against which it must struggle."

Is it really this very simple principle which emerges from the observation of social animals and human societies? Is it applicable? And how does this principle pass into a habit and continually develop? This is what we are now going to see.

V

The idea of good and evil exists within humanity itself. Man, whatever degree of intellectual development he may have attained, however his ideas may be obscured by prejudices and personal interest in general, considers as good that which is useful to the society wherein he lives, and as evil that which is hurtful to it.

But whence comes this conception, often so vague that it can scarcely be distinguished from a feeling? There are millions and millions of human beings who have never reflected about the human race. They know for the most part only the clan or family, rarely the nation, still more rarely mankind. How can it be that they should consider what is useful for the human race as good, or even attain a feeling of solidarity with their clan, in spite of all their narrow, selfish interests?

This fact has greatly occupied thinkers at all times, and it continues to occupy them still. We are going in our turn to give our view of the matter. But let us remark in passing that though the explanations of the fact may vary, the fact itself remains none the less incontestable. And should our explanation not be the true one, or should it be incomplete, the fact with its consequences to humanity will still remain. We may not be able fully to explain the origin of the planets revolving round the sun, but the planets revolve none the less, and one of them carries us with it in space.

We have already spoken of the religious explanation. If man distinguishes between good and evil, say theologians, it is God who has inspired him with this idea. Useful or hurtful is not for him to inquire; he must merely obey the fiat of his creator. We will not stop at this explanation, fruit of the ignorance and terrors of the savage. We pass on.

Others have tried to explain the fact by law. It must have been law that developed in man the sense of just and unjust, right and wrong. Our readers may judge of this explanation for themselves. They know that law has merely utilized the social feelings of man, to slip in, among the moral precepts he accepts, various mandates useful to an exploiting minority, to which his nature refuses obedience. Law has perverted the feeling of justice instead of developing it. Again let us pass on.

Neither let us pause at the explanation of the Utilitarians. They will have it that man acts morally from self-interest, and they forget his feelings of solidarity with the whole race, which exist, whatever be their origin. There is some truth in the Utilitarian explanation. But it is not the whole truth. Therefore, let us go further.

It is again to the thinkers of the eighteenth century that we are indebted for having guessed, in part at all events, the origin of the moral sentiment.

In a fine work, *The Theory of Moral Sentiment*, left to slumber in silence by religious prejudice, and indeed but little known even among anti-religious thinkers, Adam Smith has laid his finger on the true origin of the moral sentiment. He does not seek it in mystic religious feelings; he finds it simply in the feeling of sympathy.

You see a man beat a child. You know that the beaten child suffers. Your imagination causes you yourself to suffer the pain inflicted upon the child; or perhaps its tears, its little suffering face tell you. And if you are not a coward, you rush at the brute who is beating it and rescue it from him.

This example by itself explains almost all the moral sentiments. The more powerful your imagination, the better you can picture to yourself what any being feels when it is made to suffer, and the more intense and delicate will your moral sense be. The more you are drawn to put yourself in the place of the other person, the more you feel the pain inflicted upon him, the insult offered him, the injustice of which he is a victim, the more will you be urged to act so that you may prevent the pain, insult, or injustice. And the more you are accustomed by circumstances, by those surrounding you, or by the intensity of your own thought and your own imagination, to act as your thought and imagination urge, the more will the moral sentiment grow in you, the more will it become habitual.

This is what Adam Smith develops with a wealth of examples. He was young when he wrote this book, which is far superior to the work of his old age upon political economy. Free from religious prejudice, he sought the explanation of morality in a physical fact of human nature, and this is why official and non-official theological prejudice has put the treatise on the Black List for a century.

Adam Smith's only mistake was not to have understood that this same feeling of sympathy in its habitual stage exists among animals as well as among men.

The feeling of solidarity is the leading characteristic of all animals living in society. The eagle devours the sparrow, the wolf devours the marmot. But the eagles and the wolves respectively aid each other in hunting, the sparrow and the marmot unite among themselves against the beasts and birds of prey so effectually that only the very clumsy ones are caught. In all animal societies solidarity is a natural law of far greater importance than that struggle for existence, the virtue of which is sung by the ruling classes in every strain that may best serve to stultify us.

When we study the animal world and try to explain to ourselves that struggle for existence maintained by each living being against adverse circumstances and against its enemies, we realize that the more the principles of solidarity and equality are developed in an animal society and have become habitual to it, the more chance has it of surviving and coming triumphantly out of the struggle against hardships and foes. The more thoroughly each member of the society feels his solidarity with each other member of the society, the more completely are developed in all of them those two qualities which are the main factors of all progress: courage on the one hand, and on the other, free individual initiative. And on the contrary, the more any animal society or little group of animals loses this feeling of solidarity—which may chance as the result of exceptional scarcity or else of exceptional plenty—the more do the two other factors of progress courage and individual initiative, diminish. In the end they disappear, and the society falls into decay and sinks before its foes. Without mutual confidence no struggle is possible; there is no courage, no initiative, no solidarity—and no victory! Defeat is certain.

We can prove with a wealth of examples how in the animal and human worlds the law of mutual aid is the law of progress, and how mutual aid with the courage and individual initiative which follow from it secures victory to the species most capable of practicing it.

Now let us imagine this feeling of solidarity acting during the millions of ages which have succeeded one another since the first beginnings of animal life appeared upon the globe. Let us imagine how this feeling little by little became a habit, and was transmitted by heredity from the simplest microscopic organism to its descendants—

insects, birds, reptiles, mammals, man—and we shall comprehend the origin of the moral sentiment, which is a necessity to the animal like food or the organ for digesting it.

Without going further back and speaking of complex animals springing from colonies of extremely simple little beings, here is the origin of the moral sentiment. We have been obliged to be extremely brief in order to compress this great question within the limits of a few pages, but enough has already been said to show that there is nothing mysterious or sentimental about it. Without this solidarity of the individual with the species, the animal kingdom would never have developed or reached its present perfection. The most advanced being upon the earth would still be one of those tiny specks swimming in the water and scarcely perceptible under a microscope. Would even this exist? For are not the earliest aggregations of cellules themselves an instance of association in the struggle?

VI

Thus by an unprejudiced observation of the animal kingdom, we reach the conclusion that wherever society exists at all, this principle may be found: Treat others as you would like them to treat you under similar circumstances.

And when we study closely the evolution of the animal world, we discover that the aforesaid principle, translated by the one word Solidarity, has played an infinitely larger part in the development of the animal kingdom than all the adaptations that have resulted from a struggle between individuals to acquire personal advantages.

It is evident that in human societies a still greater degree of solidarity is to be met with. Even the societies of monkeys highest in the animal scale offer a striking example of practical solidarity, and man has taken a step further in the same direction. This and this alone has enabled him to preserve his puny race amid the obstacles cast by nature in his way, and to develop his intelligence.

A careful observation of those primitive societies still remaining at the level of the Stone Age shows to what a great extent the members of the same community practice solidarity among themselves.

This is the reason why practical solidarity never ceases; not even during the worst periods of history. Even when temporary circumstances of domination, servitude, exploitation cause the principle to be disowned, it still lives deep in the thoughts of the many, ready to bring about a strong recoil against evil institutions, a revolution. If it were otherwise society would perish.

For the vast majority of animals and men this feeling remains, and must remain, an acquired habit, a principle always present to the mind even when it is continually ignored in action.

It is the whole evolution of the animal kingdom speaking in us. And this evolution has lasted long, very long. It counts by hundreds of millions of years.

Even if we wished to get rid of it we could not. It would be easier for a man to accustom himself to walk on all fours than to get rid of the moral sentiment. It is anterior in animal evolution to the upright posture of man.

The moral sense is a natural faculty in us, like the sense of smell or of touch.

As for law and religion, which also have preached this principle, they have simply filched it to cloak their own wares, their injunctions for the benefit of the conqueror, the exploiter, the priest. Without this principle of solidarity, the justice of which is so generally recognized, how could they have laid hold on men's minds?

Each of them covered themselves with it as with a garment; like authority which made good its position by posing as the protector of the weak against the strong.

By flinging overboard law, religion and authority, mankind can regain possession of the moral principle which has been taken from them. Regain that they may criticize it, and purge it from the adulterations wherewith priest, judge and ruler have poisoned it and are poisoning it yet.

Besides this principle of treating others as one wishes to be treated oneself, what is it but the very same principle as equality, the fundamental principle of anarchism? And how can any one manage to believe himself an anarchist unless he practices it?

We do not wish to be ruled. And by this very fact, do we not declare that we ourselves wish to rule nobody? We do not wish to be deceived, we wish always to be told nothing but the truth. And by this very fact, do we not declare that we ourselves do not wish to deceive anybody, that we promise to always tell the truth, nothing but the truth, the whole truth? We do not wish to have the fruits of our labor stolen from us. And by that very fact, do we not declare that we respect the fruits of others' labor?

By what right indeed can we demand that we should be treated in one fashion, reserving it to ourselves to treat others in a fashion entirely different? Our sense of equality revolts at such an idea.

Equality in mutual relations with the solidarity arising from it, this is the most powerful weapon of the animal world in the struggle for existence. And equality is equity.

By proclaiming ourselves anarchists, we proclaim beforehand that we disavow any way of treating others in which we should not like them to treat us; that we will no longer tolerate the inequality that has allowed some among us to use their strength, their cunning or their ability after a fashion in which it would annoy us to have such qualities used against ourselves. Equality in all things, the synonym of equity, this is anarchism in very deed. It is not only against the abstract trinity of law, religion, and authority that we declare war. By becoming anarchists we declare war against all this wave of deceit, cunning, exploitation, depravity, vice — in a word, inequality — which they have poured into all our hearts. We declare war against their way of acting, against their way of thinking. The governed, the deceived, the exploited, the prostitute, wound above all else our sense of equality. It is in the name of equality that we are determined to have no more prostituted, exploited, deceived and governed men and women.

Perhaps it may be said — it has been said sometimes — "But if you think that you must always treat others as you would be treated yourself, what right have you to use force under any circumstances whatever? What right have you to level a cannon at any barbarous or civilized invaders of your country? What right have you to dispossess the exploiter? What right to kill not only a tyrant but a mere viper?"

What right? What do you mean by that singular word, borrowed from the law? Do you wish to know if I shall feel conscious of having acted well in doing this? If those I esteem will think I have done well? Is this what you ask? If so the answer is simple.

Yes, certainly! Because we ourselves should ask to be killed like venomous beasts if we went to invade Burmese or Zulus who have done us no harm. We should say to our son or our friend: "Kill me, if I ever take part in the invasion!"

Yes, certainly! Because we ourselves should ask to be dispossessed, if, giving the lie to our principles, we seized upon an inheritance, did it fall from on high, to use it for the exploitation of others.

Yes, certainly! Because any man with a heart asks beforehand that he may be slain if ever he becomes venomous; that a dagger may be plunged into his heart if ever he should take the place of a dethroned tyrant.

Ninety-nine men out of a hundred who have a wife and children would try to commit suicide for fear they should do harm to those they love, if they felt themselves going mad. Whenever a good-hearted man feels himself becoming dangerous to those he loves, he wishes to die before he is so.

Perovskaya and her comrades killed the Russian Czar. And all mankind, despite the repugnance to the spilling of blood, despite the sympathy for one who had allowed the serfs to be liberated, recognized their right to do as they did. Why? Not because the act was generally recognized as useful; two out of three still doubt if it were so. But because it was felt that not for all the gold in the world would Perovskaya and her comrades have consented to become tyrants themselves. Even those who know nothing of the drama are certain that it was no youthful bravado, no palace conspiracy, no attempt to gain power. It was hatred of tyranny, even to the scorn of self, even to the death.

"These men and women," it was said, "had conquered the right to kill"; as it was said of Louise Michel, "She had the right to rob." Or again, "They have the right to steal," in speaking of those terrorists who lived on dry bread, and stole a million or two of the Kishineff treasure.

Mankind has never refused the right to use force on those who have conquered that right, be it exercised upon the barricades or in the shadow of a cross-way. But if such an act is to produce a deep impression upon men's minds, the right must be conquered. Without this, such an act whether useful or not will remain merely a brutal fact, of no importance in the progress of ideas. People will see in it nothing but a displacement of force, simply the substitution of one exploiter for another.

VII

We have hitherto been speaking of the conscious, deliberate actions of man, those performed intentionally. But side by side with our conscious life we have an unconscious life which is very much wider. Yet we have only to notice how we dress in the morning, trying to fasten a button that we know we lost last night, or stretching out our hand to take something that we ourselves have moved away, to obtain an idea of this unconscious life and realize the enormous part it plays in our existence.

It makes up three-fourths of our relations with others. Our ways of speaking, smiling, frowning, getting heated or keeping cool in a discussion, are unintentional, the result of habits, inherited from our human or pre-human ancestors (only notice the likeness in expression between an angry man and an angry beast), or else consciously or unconsciously acquired.

Our manner of acting towards others thus tends to become habitual. To treat others as he would wish to be treated himself becomes with man and all sociable animals, simply a habit. So much so that a person does not generally even ask himself how he must act under such and such circumstances. It is only when the circumstances are exceptional, in some complex case or under the impulse of strong passion that he hesitates, and a struggle takes place between the various portions of his brain—for the brain is a very complex organ, the various portions of which act to a certain degree independently. When this happens, the man substitutes himself in imagination for the person opposed to him; he asks himself if he would like to be treated in such a way, and the better he has identified himself with the person whose dignity or interests he has been on the point of injuring, the more moral will his decision be. Or maybe a friend steps in and says to him: "Fancy yourself in his place; should you have suffered from being treated by him as he has been treated by you?" And this is enough. Thus we only appeal to the principle of equality in moments of hesitation, and in ninety-nine cases out of a hundred act morally from habit.

It must have been obvious that in all we have hitherto said, we have not attempted to enjoin anything, we have only set forth the manner in which things happen in the animal world and amongst mankind.

Formerly the church threatened men with hell to moralize them, and she succeeded in demoralizing them instead. The judge threatens with imprisonment, flogging, the gallows, in the name of those social principles he has filched from society; and he demoralizes them. And yet the very idea that the judge may disappear from the earth at the same time as the priest causes authoritarians of every shade to cry out about peril to society.

But we are not afraid to forego judges and their sentences. We forego sanctions of all kinds, even obligations to morality. We are not afraid to say: "Do what you will; act as you will"; because we are persuaded that the great majority of mankind, in proportion to their degree of enlightenment and the completeness with which they free themselves from existing fetters, will behave and act always in a direction useful to society, just as we are persuaded beforehand that a child will one day walk on its two feet and not on all fours simply because it is born of parents belonging to the genus *Homo*.

All we can do is to give advice. And again while giving it we add: "This advice will be valueless if your own experience and observation do not lead you to recognize that it is worth following."

When we see a youth stooping and so contracting his chest and lungs we advise him to straighten himself, hold up his head and open his chest. We advise him to fill his lungs and take long breaths, because this will be his best safeguard against consumption. But at the same time we teach him physiology that he may understand the functions of his lungs, and himself choose the posture he knows to be the best.

And this is all we can do in the case of morals. We have only a right to give advice, to which we add: "Follow it if it seems good to you."

But while leaving to each the right to act as he thinks best; while utterly denying the right of society to punish one in any way for any anti-social act he may have committed, we do not forego our own capacity to love what seems to us good and to hate what seems to us bad. Love and hate; for only those who know how to hate know how to love. We keep this capacity; and as this alone serves to maintain and develop the moral sentiments in every animal society, so much the more will it be enough for the human race.

We only ask one thing, to eliminate all that impedes the free development of these two feelings in the present society, all that perverts our judgment—the State, the church, exploitation, judges, priests, governments, exploiters.

Today when we see a Jack the Ripper murder one after another some of the poorest and most miserable of women, our first feeling is one of hatred.

If we had met him the day when he murdered that woman who asked him to pay her for her slum lodging, we should have put a bullet through his head, without reflecting that the bullet might have been better bestowed in the brain of the owner of that wretched den.

But when we recall to mind all the infamies which have brought him to this; when we think of the darkness in which he prowls haunted by images drawn from indecent books or thoughts suggested by stupid books, our feeling is divided. And if some day we hear that Jack is in the hands of some judge who has slain in cold blood a far greater number of men, women and children than all the Jacks together; if we see him in the hands of one of those deliberate maniacs then all our hatred of Jack the Ripper will vanish. It will be transformed into hatred of a cowardly and hypocritical society and its recognized representatives. All the infamies of a Ripper disappear before that long series of infamies committed in the name of law. It is these we hate.

At the present day our feelings are continually thus divided. We feel that all of us are more or less, voluntarily or involuntarily, abettors of this society. We do not dare to hate. Do we even dare to love? In a society based on exploitation and servitude human nature is degraded.

But as servitude disappears we shall regain our rights. We shall feel within ourselves strength to hate and to love, even in such complicated cases as that we have just cited.

In our daily life we do already give free scope to our feelings of sympathy or antipathy; we are doing so every moment. We all love moral strength; we all despise moral weakness and cowardice. Every moment our words, looks, smiles express our joy in seeing actions useful to the human race, those which we think good. Every moment our looks and words show the repugnance we feel towards cowardice, deceit, intrigue, want of moral courage. We betray our disgust, even when under the influence of a worldly education we try to hide our contempt beneath those lying appearances which will vanish as equal relations are established among us.

This alone is enough to keep the conception of good and ill at a certain level and to communicate it one to another.

It will be still more efficient when there is no longer judge or priest in society, when moral principles have lost their obligatory character and are considered merely as relations between equals.

Moreover, in proportion to the establishment of these relations, a loftier moral conception will arise in society. It is this conception which we are about to analyze.

VIII

Thus far our analysis has only set forth the simple principles of equality. We have revolted and invited others to revolt against those who assume the right to treat their fellows otherwise than they would be treated themselves; against those who, not themselves wishing to be deceived, exploited, prostituted or ill-used, yet behave thus to others. Lying, and brutality are repulsive, we have said, not because they are disapproved by codes of morality, but because such conduct revolts the sense of equality in everyone to whom equality is not an empty word. And above all does it revolt him who is a true anarchist in his way of thinking and acting.

If nothing but this simple, natural, obvious principle were generally applied in life, a very lofty morality would be the result; a morality comprising all that moralists have taught.

The principle of equality sums up the teachings of moralists. But it also contains something more. This something more is respect for the individual. By proclaiming our morality of equality, or anarchism, we refuse to assume a right which moralists have always taken upon themselves to claim, that of mutilating the individual in the name of some ideal. We do not recognize this right at all, for ourselves or anyone else. We recognize the full and complete liberty of the individual; we desire for him plentitude of existence, the free development of all his faculties. We wish to impose nothing upon him; thus returning to the principle which Fourier placed in opposition to religious morality when he said:

"Leave men absolutely free. Do not mutilate them, as religions have done enough and to spare. Do not fear even their passions. In a free society these are not dangerous."

Provided that you yourself do not abdicate your freedom, provided that you yourself do not allow others to enslave you; and provided that to the violent and anti-social passions of this or that person you oppose your equally vigorous social passions, you have nothing to fear from liberty.

We renounce the idea of mutilating the individual in the name of any ideal whatsoever. All we reserve to ourselves is the frank expression of our sympathies and antipathies towards what seems to us good or bad. A man deceives his friends. It is his bent, his character to do so. Very well, it is our character, our bent to despise liars. And as this is our character, let us be frank. Do not let us rush and press him to our bosom or cordially shake hands with him, as is sometimes done today. Let us vigorously oppose our active passion to his.

This is all we have the right to do, this is all the duty we have to perform to keep up the principle of equality in society. It is the principle of equality in practice.

But what of the murderer, the man who debauches children? The murderer who kills from sheer thirst for blood is excessively rare. He is a madman to be cured or avoided. As for the debauchee, let us first of all look to it that society does not pervert our children's feelings, then we shall have little to fear from rakes.

All this it must be understood is not completely applicable until the great sources of moral depravity—capitalism, religion, justice, government—shall have ceased to exist. But the greater part of it may be put in practice from this day forth. It is in practice already.

And yet if societies knew only this principle of equality; if each man practiced merely the equity of a trader, taking care all day long not to give others anything more than he was receiving from them, society would die of it. The very principle of equality itself would disappear from our relations. For, if it is to be maintained, something grander, more lovely, more vigorous than mere equity must perpetually find a place in life. And this greater than justice is here.

Until now humanity has never been without large natures overflowing with tenderness, with intelligence, with goodwill, and using their feeling, their intellect, their active force in the service of the human race without asking anything in return.

This fertility of mind, of feeling or of goodwill, takes all possible forms. It is in the passionate seeker after truth, who renounces all other pleasures to throw his energy into the search for what he believes true and right, contrary to the affirmations of the ignoramuses around him. It is in the inventor who lives from day to day forgetting even his food, scarcely touching the bread with which perhaps some woman devoted to him feeds him like a child, while he follows out the intention he thinks destined to change the face of the world. It is in the ardent revolutionist to whom the joys of art, of science, even of family life, seem bitter, so long as they cannot be shared by all, and who works despite misery and persecution for the regeneration of the world. It is in the youth who, hearing of the atrocities of invasion, and taking literally the heroic legends of patriotism, inscribes himself in a volunteer corps and marches bravely through snow and hunger until he falls beneath the bullets. It was in the Paris street urchin, with his quick intelligence and bright choice of aversions and sympathies, who ran to the ramparts with his little brother, stood steady amid the rain of shells, and died murmuring: "Long live the Commune!" It is in the man who is revolted at the sight of a wrong without waiting to ask what will be its result to himself, and when all backs are bent stands up to unmask the iniquity and brand the exploiter, the petty despot of a factory or great tyrant of an empire. Finally it is in all those numberless acts of devotion less striking and therefore unknown and almost always misprized, which may be continually observed, especially among women, if we will take the trouble to open our eyes and notice what lies at the very foundation of human life, and enables it to enfold itself one way or another in spite of the exploitation and oppression it undergoes.

Such men and women as these, some in obscurity, some within a larger arena, creates the progress of mankind. And mankind is aware of it. This is why it encompasses such lives with reverence, with myths. It adorns them, makes them the subject of its stories, songs, romances. It adores in them the courage, goodness, love and devotion which are lacking in most of us. It transmits their memory to the young. It recalls even those who have acted only in the narrow circle of home and friends, and reveres their memory in family tradition.

Such men and women as these make true morality, the only morality worthy the name. All the rest is merely equality in relations. Without their courage, their devotion, humanity would remain besotted in the mire of petty calculations. It is such men and women as these who prepare the morality of the future, that which will come when our children have ceased to reckon, and have grown up to the idea that the best use for all energy, courage and love is to expend it where the need of such a force is most strongly felt.

Such courage, such devotion has existed in every age. It is to be met with among sociable animals. It is to be found among men, even during the most degraded epochs.

And religions have always sought to appropriate it, to turn it into current coin for their own benefit. In fact if religions are still alive, it is because—ignorance apart—they have always appealed to this very devotion and courage. And it is to this that revolutionists appeal.

The moral sentiment of duty which each man has felt in his life, and which it has been attempted to explain by every sort of mysticism, the unconsciously anarchist Guyau says, "is nothing but a superabundance of life, which demands to be exercised, to give itself; at the same time, it is the consciousness of a power."

All accumulated force creates a pressure upon the obstacles placed before it. Power to act is duty to act. And moral "obligation" of which so much has been said or written is reduced to the conception: the condition of the maintenance of life is its expansion.

"The plant cannot prevent itself from flowering. Sometimes to flower means to die. Never mind, the sap mounts the same," concludes the young anarchist philosopher.

It is the same with the human being when he is full of force and energy. Force accumulates in him. He expands his life. He gives without calculation, otherwise he could not live. If he must die like the flower when it blooms, never mind. The sap rises, if sap there be.

Be strong. Overflow with emotional and intellectual energy, and you will spread your intelligence, your love, your energy of action broadcast among others! This is what all moral teaching comes to.

IX

That which mankind admires in a truly moral man is his energy, the exuberance of life which urges him to give his intelligence, his feeling, his action, asking nothing in return.

The strong thinker, the man overflowing with intellectual life, naturally seeks to diffuse his ideas. There is no pleasure in thinking unless the thought is communicated to others. It is only the mentally poverty-stricken man, who after he has painfully hunted up some idea, carefully hides it that later on he may label it with his own name. The man of powerful intellect runs over with ideas; he scatters them by the handful. He is wretched if he cannot share them with others, cannot scatter them to the four winds, for in this is his life.

The same with regard to feeling. "We are not enough for ourselves: we have more tears than our own sufferings claim, more capacity for joy than our own existence can justify," says Guyau, thus summing up the whole question of morality in a few admirable lines, caught from nature. The solitary being is wretched, restless, because he cannot share his thoughts and feelings with others. When we feel some great pleasure, we wish to let others know that we exist, we feel, we love, we live, we struggle, we fight.

At the same time, we feel the need to exercise our will, our active energy. To act, to work has become a need for the vast majority of mankind. So much so that when absurd conditions divorce a man or woman from useful work, they invent something to do, some futile and senseless obligations whereby to open out a field for their active energy. They invent a theory, a religion, a "social duty" — to persuade themselves that they are doing something useful. When they dance, it is for a charity. When they ruin themselves with expensive dresses, it is to keep up the position of the aristocracy. When they do nothing, it is on principle.

"We need to help our fellows, to lend a hand to the coach laboriously dragged along by humanity; in any case, we buzz round it," says Guyau. This need of lending a hand is so great that it is found among all sociable animals, however low in the scale. What is all the enormous amount of activity spent uselessly in politics every day but an expression of the need to lend a hand to the coach of humanity, or at least to buzz around it.

Of course this "fecundity of will," this thirst for action, when accompanied by poverty of feeling and an intellect incapable of creation, will produce nothing but a Napoleon I or a Bismarck, wiseacres who try to force the world to progress backwards. While on the other hand, mental fertility destitute of well developed sensibility will bring forth such barren fruits as literary and scientific pedants who only hinder the advance of knowledge. Finally, sensibility unguided by large intelligence will produce such persons as the woman ready to sacrifice everything for some brute of a man, upon whom she pours forth all her love.

If life to be really fruitful, it must be so at once in intelligence, in feeling and in will. This fertility in every direction is life; the only thing worthy the name. For one moment of this life, those who have obtained a glimpse of it give years of vegetative existence. Without this overflowing life, a man is old before his time, an impotent being, a plant that withers before it has ever flowered.

"Let us leave to latter-day corruption this life that is no life," cries youth, the true youth full of sap that longs to live and scatter life around. Every time a society falls into decay, a thrust from such youth as this shatters ancient economic, and political and moral forms to make room for the up-springing of a new life. What matter if one or another fall in the struggle! Still the sap rises. For youth to live is to blossom whatever the consequences! It does not regret them.

But without speaking of the heroic periods of mankind, taking every-day existence, is it life to live in disagreement with one's ideal?

Now-a-days it is often said that men scoff at the ideal. And it is easy to understand why. The word has so often been used to cheat the simple-hearted that a reaction is inevitable and healthy. We too should like to replace the word "ideal," so often blotted and stained, by a new word more in conformity with new ideas.

But whatever the word, the fact remains; every human being has his ideal. Bismarck had his—however strange—a government of blood and iron. Even every philistine has his ideal, however low.

But besides these, there is the human being who has conceived a loftier ideal. The life of a beast cannot satisfy him. Servility, lying, bad faith, intrigue, inequality in human relations fill him with loathing. How can he in his turn become servile, be a liar, and intriguer, lord it over others? He catches a glimpse of how lovely life might be if better relations existed among men; he feels in himself the power to succeed in establishing these better relations with those he may meet on his way. He conceives what is called an ideal.

Whence comes this ideal? How is it fashioned by heredity on one side and the impressions of life on the other? We know not. At most we could tell the story of it more or less truly in our own biographies. But it is an actual fact—variable, progressive, open to outside influences but always living. It is a largely unconscious feeling of what would give the greatest amount of vitality, of the joy of life.

Life is vigorous, fertile, rich in sensation only on condition of answering to this feeling of the ideal. Act against this feeling, and you feel your life bent back on itself. It is no longer at one, it loses its vigor. Be untrue often to your ideal and you will end by paralyzing your will, your active energy. Soon you will no longer regain the vigor, the spontaneity of decision you formerly knew. You are a broken man.

Nothing mysterious in all this, once you look upon a human being as a compound of nervous and cerebral centers acting independently. Waver between the various feelings striving within you, and you will soon end by breaking the harmony of the organism; you will be a sick person without will. The intensity of your life will decrease. In vain will you seek for compromises. Never more will you be the complete, strong, vigorous being you were when your acts were in accordance with the ideal conceptions of your brain.

There are epochs in which the moral conception changes entirely. A man perceives that what he had considered moral is the deepest immorality. In some instances it is a custom, a venerated tradition, that is fundamentally immoral. In others we find a moral system framed in the interests of a single class. We cast them overboard and raise the cry "Down with morality!" It becomes a duty to act "immorally."

Let us welcome such epochs, for they are epochs of criticism. They are an infallible sign that thought is working in society. A higher morality has begun to be wrought out.

What this morality will be we have sought to formulate, taking as our basis the study of man and animal.

We have seen the kind of morality which is even now shaping itself in the ideas of the masses and of the thinkers. This morality will issue no commands. It will refuse once and for all to model individuals according to an abstract idea, as it will refuse to mutilate them by religion, law or government. It will leave to the individual man full and perfect liberty. It will be but a simple record of facts, a science. And this science will say to man: "If you are not conscious of strength within you, if your energies are only just sufficient to maintain a colorless, monotonous life, without strong impressions, without deep joys, but also without deep sorrows, well then, keep to the simple principles of a just equality. In relations of equality you will find probably the maximum of happiness possible to your feeble energies."

"But if you feel within you the strength of youth, if you wish to live, if you wish to enjoy a perfect, full and overflowing life — that is, know the highest pleasure which a living being can desire — be strong, be great, be vigorous in all you do."

"Sow life around you. Take heed that if you deceive, lie, intrigue, cheat, you thereby demean yourself, belittle yourself, confess your own weakness beforehand, play the part of the slave of the harem who feels himself the inferior of his master. Do this if it so pleases you, but know that humanity will regard you as petty, contemptible and feeble, and treat you as such. Having no evidence of your strength, it will act towards you as one worthy of pity — and pity only. Do not blame humanity if of your own accord you thus paralyze your energies. Be strong on the other hand, and once you have seen unrighteousness and recognized it as such — inequity in life, a lie in science, or suffering inflicted by another — rise in revolt against the iniquity, the lie or the injustice. "Struggle! To struggle is to live, and the fiercer the struggle the intenser the life. Then you will have lived; and a few hours of such life are worth years spent vegetating."

"Struggle so that all may live this rich, overflowing life. And be sure that in this struggle you will find a joy greater than anything else can give." This is all that the science of morality can tell you. Yours is the choice.

Anarchism: Its Philosophy and Ideal

1898

(Editor's Note: A good summary of the anarchist outlook.)

Ever reviled, accursed, n'er understood, Thou art the grisly terror of our age. "Wreck of all order," cry the multitude, "Art thou, and war and murder's endless rage." O, let them cry. To them that ne'er have striven, The truth that lies behind a word to find, To them the word's right meaning was not given. They shall continue blind among the blind. But thou, O word, so clear, so strong, so pure, That sayest all which I for goal have taken. I give thee to the future! Thine secure When each at last unto himself shall waken. Comes it in sunshine? In the tempest's thrill? I cannot tell......but it the earth shall see! I am an Anarchist! Wherefore I will not rule, and also ruled I will not be!

— John Henry Mackay.

It is not without a certain hesitation that I have decided to take the philosophy and ideal of Anarchy as the subject of this lecture.

Those who are persuaded that Anarchy is a collection of visions relating to the future, and an unconscious striving toward the destruction of all present civilization, are still very numerous; and to clear the ground of such prejudices of our education as maintain this view we should have, perhaps, to enter into many details which it would be difficult to embody in a single lecture. Did not the Parisian press, only two or three years ago, maintain that the whole philosophy of Anarchy consisted in destruction, and that its only argument was violence?

Nevertheless Anarchists have been spoken of so much lately, that part of the public has at last taken to reading and discussing our doctrines. Sometimes men have even given themselves trouble to reflect, and at the present moment we have at least gained a point: it is willingly admitted that Anarchists have an ideal. Their ideal is even found too beautiful, too lofty for a society not composed of superior beings.

But is it not pretentious on my part to speak of a philosophy, when, according to our critics, our ideas are but dim visions of a distant future? Can Anarchy pretend to possess a philosophy, when it is denied that Socialism has one?

This is what I am about to answer with all possible precision and clearness, only asking you to excuse me beforehand if I repeat an example or two which I have already given at a London lecture, and which seem to be best fitted to explain what is meant by the philosophy of Anarchism.

You will not bear me any ill-will if I begin by taking a few elementary illustrations borrowed from natural sciences. Not for the purpose of deducing our social ideas from them—far from it; but simply the better to set off certain relations, which are easier grasped in phenomena verified by the exact sciences than in examples only taken from the complex facts of human societies.

Well, then, what especially strikes us at present in exact sciences, is the profound modification which they are undergoing now, in the whole of their conceptions and interpretations of the facts of the universe.

There was a time, you know, when man imagined the earth placed in the center of the universe. Sun, moon, planets and stars seemed to roll round our globe; and this globe, inhabited by man, represented for him the center of creation. He himself—the superior being on his planet—was the elected of his Creator. The sun, the moon, the stars were but made for him; toward him was directed all the attention of a God, who watched the least of his actions, arrested the sun's course for him, wafted in the clouds, launching his showers or his thunder-bolts on fields and cities, to recompense the virtue or punish the crimes of mankind. For thousands of years man thus conceived the universe.

You know also what an immense change was produced in the sixteenth century in all conceptions of the civilized part of mankind, when it was demonstrated that, far from being the centre of the universe, the earth was only a grain of sand in the solar system—a ball, much smaller even than the other planets; that the sun itself, though immense in comparison to our little earth, was but a star among many other countless stars which we see shining in the skies and swarming in the milky-way. How small man appeared in comparison to this immensity without limits, how ridiculous his pretensions! All the philosophy of that epoch, all social and religious conceptions, felt the effects of this transformation in cosmogony. Natural science, whose present development we are so proud of, only dates from that time.

But a change, much more profound, and with far wider reaching results, is being effected at the present time in the whole of the sciences, and Anarchy, you will see, is but one of the many manifestations of this evolution.

Take any work on astronomy of the last century, or the beginning of ours. You will no longer find in it, it goes without saying, our tiny planet placed in the center of the universe. But you will meet at every step the idea of a central luminary—the sun—which by its powerful attraction governs our planetary world. From this central body radiates a force guiding the course of the planets, and maintaining the harmony of the system. Issued from a central agglomeration, planets have, so to say, budded from it; they owe their birth to this agglomeration; they owe everything to the radiant star that represents it still: the rhythm of their movements, their orbits set at wisely regulated distances, the life that animates them and adorns their surfaces. And when any perturbation disturbs their course and makes them deviate from their orbits, the central body re-establishes order in the system; it assures and perpetuates its existence.

This conception, however, is also disappearing as the other one did. After having fixed all their attention on the sun and the large planets, astronomers are beginning to study now the infinitely small ones that people the universe. And they discover that the interplanetary and interstellar spaces are peopled and crossed in all imaginable directions by little swarms of matter, invisible, infinitely small when taken separately, but all-powerful in their numbers. Among those masses, some, like the bolide that fell in Spain some time ago, are still rather big; others weigh but a few ounces or grains, while around them is wafted dust, almost microscopic, filling up the spaces.

It is to this dust, to these infinitely tiny bodies that dash through space in all directions with giddy swiftness, that clash with one another, agglomerate, disintegrate, everywhere and always, it is to them that today astronomers look for an explanation of the origin of our solar system, the movements that animate its parts, and the harmony of their whole. Yet another step, and soon universal gravitation itself will be but the result of all the disordered and incoherent movements of these infinitely small bodies—of oscillations of atoms that manifest themselves in all possible directions. Thus the center, the origin of force, formerly transferred from the earth to the sun, now turns out to be scattered and disseminated: it is everywhere and nowhere. With the astronomer, we perceive that solar systems are the work of infinitely small bodies; that the power which was supposed to govern the system is itself but the result of the collisions among those infinitely tiny clusters of matter, that the harmony of stellar systems is harmony only because it is an adaptation, a resultant of all these numberless movements uniting, completing, equilibrating one another.

The whole aspect of the universe changes with this new conception. The idea of force governing the world, of pre-established law, preconceived harmony, disappears to make room for the harmony that Fourier had caught a glimpse of: the one which results from the disorderly and incoherent movements of numberless hosts of matter, each of which goes its own way and all of which hold each other in equilibrium.

If it were only astronomy that were undergoing this change! But no; the same modification takes place in the philosophy of all sciences without exception; those which study nature as well as those which study human relations.

In physical sciences, the entities of heat, magnetism, and electricity disappear. When a physicist speaks today of a heated or electrified body, he no longer sees an inanimate mass, to which an unknown force should be added. He strives to recognize in this body and in the surrounding space, the course, the vibrations of infinitely small atoms which dash in all directions, vibrate, move, live, and by their vibrations, their shocks, their life, produce the phenomena of heat, light, magnetism or electricity.

In sciences that treat of organic life, the notion of species and its variations is being substituted by a notion of the variations of the individual. The botanist and zoologist study the individual—his life, his adaptations to his surroundings. Changes produced in him by the action of drought or damp, heat or cold, abundance or poverty of nourishment, of his more or less sensitiveness to the action of exterior surroundings will originate species; and the variations of species are now for the biologist but resultants—a given sum of variations that have been produced in each individual separately. A species will be what the individuals are, each undergoing numberless influences from the surroundings in which they live, and to which they correspond each in his own way.

And when a physiologist speaks now of the life of a plant or of an animal, he sees rather an agglomeration, a colony of millions of separate individuals, than a personality one and indivisible. He speaks of a federation of digestive, sensual, nervous organs, all very intimately connected with one another, each feeling the consequence of the well-being or indisposition of each, but each living its own life. Each organ, each part of an organ in its turn, is composed of independent cellules which associate to struggle against conditions unfavorable to their existence. The individual is quite a world of federations, a whole universe in himself.

And in this world of aggregated beings the physiologist sees the autonomous cells of blood, of the tissues, of the nerve-centers; he recognizes the millions of white corpuscles—the phagocytes—who wend their way to the parts of the body infected by microbes in order to give battle to the invaders. More than that: in each microscopic cell he discovers today a world of autonomous organisms, each of which lives its own life, looks for well-being for itself and attains it by grouping and associating itself with others. In short, each individual is a cosmos of organs, each organ is a cosmos of cells, each cell is a cosmos of infinitely small ones; and in this complex world, the well-being of the whole depends entirely on the sum of well-being enjoyed by each of the least microscopic particles of organized matter. A whole revolution is thus produced in the philosophy of life.

But it is especially in psychology that this revolution leads to consequences of great importance.

Quite recently the psychologist spoke of man as an entire being, one and indivisible. Remaining faithful to religious tradition, he used to class men as good and bad, intelligent and stupid, egotists and altruists. Even with materialists of the eighteenth century, the idea of a soul, of an indivisible entity, was still upheld.

But what would we think today of a psychologist who would still speak like this! The modern psychologist sees in man a multitude of separate faculties, autonomous tendencies, equal among themselves, performing their functions independently, balancing, opposing one another continually. Taken as a whole, man is nothing but a resultant, always changeable, of all his diverse faculties, of all his autonomous tendencies, of brain cells and nerve centers. All are related so closely to one another that they each react on all the others, but they lead their own life without being subordinated to a central organ—the soul.

Without entering into further details you thus see that a profound modification is being produced at this moment in the whole of natural sciences. Not that this analysis is extended to details formerly neglected. No! The facts are not new, but the way of looking at them is in course of evolution; and if we had to characterize this tendency in a few words, we might say that if formerly science strove to study the results and the great sums (integrals, as mathematicians say), today it strives to study the infinitely small ones—the individuals of which those sums are composed and in which it now recognizes independence and individuality at the same time as this intimate aggregation.

As to the harmony that the human mind discovers in Nature, and which harmony is, on the whole, but the verification of a certain stability of phenomena, the modern man of science no doubt recognizes it more than ever. But he no longer tries to explain it by the action of laws conceived according to a certain plan pre-established by an intelligent will.

What used to be called "natural law" is nothing but a certain relation among phenomena which we dimly see, and each "law" takes a temporary character of causality; that is to say: If such a phenomenon is produced under such conditions, such another phenomenon will follow. No law placed outside the phenomena: each phenomenon governs that which follows it — not law.

Nothing preconceived in what we call harmony in Nature. The chance of collisions and encounters has sufficed to establish it. Such a phenomenon will last for centuries because the adaptation, the equilibrium it represents, has taken centuries to be established; while such another will last but an instant if that form of momentary equilibrium was born in an instant. If the planets of our solar system do not collide with one another and do not destroy one another every day, if they last millions of years, it is because they represent an equilibrium that has taken millions of centuries to establish as a resultant of millions of blind forces. If continents are not continually destroyed by volcanic shocks, it is because they have taken thousands and thousands of centuries to build up, molecule by molecule, and to take their present shape. But lightning will only last an instant; because it represents a momentary rupture of the equilibrium, a sudden redistribution of force.

Harmony thus appears as a temporary adjustment, established among all forces acting upon a given spot — a provisory adaptation; and that adjustment will only last under one condition: that of being continually modified; of representing every moment the resultant of all conflicting actions. Let but one of those forces be hampered in its action for some time and harmony disappears. Force will accumulate its effect; it must come to light, it must exercise its action, and if other forces hinder its manifestation it will not be annihilated by that, but will end by upsetting the present adjustment, by destroying harmony, in order to find a new form of equilibrium and to work to form a new adaptation. Such is the eruption of a volcano, whose imprisoned force ends by breaking the petrified lavas which hindered them to pour forth the gases, the molten lavas, and the incandescent ashes. Such, also, are the revolutions of mankind.

An analogous transformation is being produced at the same time in the sciences that treat of man. Thus we see that history, after having been the history of kingdoms, tends to become the history of nations and then the study of individuals. The historian wants to know how the members, of which such a nation was composed, lived at such a time, what their beliefs were, their means of existence, what ideal of society was visible to them, and what means they possessed to march toward this ideal. And by the action of all those forces, formerly neglected, he interprets the great historical phenomena.

So the man of science who studies jurisprudence is no longer content with such or such a code. Like the ethnologist he wants to know the genesis of the institution that succeed one another; he follows their evolution through ages, and in this study he applies himself far less to written law than to local customs—to the "customary law" in which the constructive genius of the unknown masses has found expression in all times. A wholly new science is being elaborated in this direction and promises to upset established conceptions we learned at school, succeeding in interpreting history in the same manner as natural sciences interpret the phenomena of Nature.

And, finally, political economy, which was at the beginning a study of the wealth of nations, becomes today a study of the wealth of individuals. It cares less to know if such a nation has or has not a large foreign trade; it wants to be assured that bread is not wanting in the peasant's or worker's cottage. It knocks at all doors—at that of the palace as well as that of the hovel—and asks the rich as well as the poor: Up to what point are your needs satisfied both for necessaries and luxuries?

And as it discovers that the most pressing needs of nine-tenths of each nation are not satisfied, it asks itself the question that a physiologist would ask himself about a plant or an animal: "Which are the means to satisfy the needs of all with the least loss of power? How can a society guarantee to each, and consequently to all, the greatest sum of satisfaction?" It is in this direction that economic science is being transformed; and after having been so long a simple statement of phenomena interpreted in the interest of a rich minority, it tends to become (or rather it elaborates the elements to become) a science in the true sense of the word—a physiology of human societies.

While a new philosophy—a new view of knowledge taken as a whole—is thus being worked out, we may observe that a different conception of society, very different from that which now prevails, is in process of formation. Under the name of Anarchy, a new interpretation of the past and present life of society arises, giving at the same time a forecast as regards its future, both conceived in the same spirit as the above-mentioned interpretation in natural sciences. Anarchy, therefore, appears as a constituent part of the new philosophy, and that is why Anarchists come in contact, on so many points, with the greatest thinkers and poets of the present day.

In fact, it is certain that in proportion as the human mind frees itself from ideas inculcated by minorities of priests, military chiefs and judges, all striving to establish their domination, and of scientists paid to perpetuate it, a conception of society arises, in which conception there is no longer room for those dominating minorities. A society entering into possession of the social capital accumulated by the labor of preceding generations, organizing itself so as to make use of this capital in the interests of all, and constituting itself without reconstituting the power of the ruling minorities. It comprises in its midst an infinite variety of capacities, temperaments and individual energies: it excludes none. It even calls for struggles and contentions; because we know that periods of contests, so long as they were freely fought out, without the weight of constituted authority being thrown on the one side of the balance, were periods when human genius took its mightiest flight and achieved the greatest aims. Acknowledging, as a fact, the equal rights of all its members to the treasures accumulated in the past, it no longer recognizes a division between exploited and exploiters, governed and governors, dominated and dominators, and it seeks to establish a certain harmonious compatibility in its midst— not by subjecting all its members to an authority that is fictitiously supposed to represent society, not by trying to establish uniformity, but by urging all men to develop free initiative, free action, free association.

It seeks the most complete development of individuality combined with the highest development of voluntary association in all its aspects, in all possible degrees, for all imaginable aims; ever changing, ever modified associations which carry in themselves the elements of their durability and constantly assume new forms, which answer best to the multiple aspirations of all.

A society to which pre-established forms, crystalized by law, are repugnant; which looks for harmony in an ever-changing and fugitive equilibrium between a multitude of varied forces and influences of every kind, following their own course—these forces promoting themselves the energies which are favorable to their march toward progress, toward the liberty of developing in broad daylight and counter-balancing one another.

This conception and ideal of society is certainly not new. On the contrary, when we analyze the history of popular institutions—the clan, the village community, the guild and even the urban commune of the Middle Ages in their first stages—we find the same popular tendency to constitute a society according to this idea; a tendency, however, always trammeled by domineering minorities. All popular movements bore this stamp more or less, and with the Anabaptists and their forerunners in the ninth century we already find the same ideas clearly expressed in the religious language which was in use at that time. Unfortunately, till the end of the last century, this ideal was always tainted by a theocratic spirit; and it is only nowadays that the conception of society deduced from the observation of social phenomena is rid of its swaddling-clothes.

It is only today that the ideal of a society where each governs himself according to his own will (which is evidently a result of the social influences borne by each) is affirmed in its economic, political and moral aspects at one and the same time, and that this ideal presents itself based on the necessity of Communism, imposed on our modern societies by the eminently social character of our present production.

In fact, we know full well today that it is futile to speak of liberty as long as economic slavery exists.

"Speak not of liberty—poverty is slavery!" is not a vain formula; it has penetrated into the ideas of the great working-class masses; it filters through all the present literature; it even carries those along who live on the poverty of others, and takes from them the arrogance with which they formerly asserted their rights to exploitation.

Millions of Socialists of both hemispheres already agree that the present form of capitalistic appropriation cannot last much longer. Capitalists themselves feel that it must go and dare not defend it with their former assurance. Their only argument is reduced to saying to us: "You have invented nothing better!" But as to denying the fatal consequences of the present forms of property, as to justifying their right to property, they cannot do it. They will practice this right as long as freedom of action is left to them, but without trying to base it on an idea. This is easily understood.

For instance, take the town of Paris—a creation of so many centuries, a product of the genius of a whole nation, a result of the labor of twenty or thirty generations. How could one maintain to an inhabitant of that town who works every day to embellish it, to purify it, to nourish it, to make it a centre of thought and art—how could one assert before one who produces this wealth that the palaces adorning the streets of Paris belong in all justice to those who are the legal proprietors today, when we are all creating their value, which would be nil without us?

Such a fiction can be kept up for some time by the skill of the people's educators. The great battalions of workers may not even reflect about it; but from the moment a minority of thinking men agitate the question and submit it to all, there can be no doubt of the result. Popular opinion answers: "It is by spoliation that they hold these riches!"

Likewise, how can the peasant be made to believe that the bourgeois or manorial land belongs to the proprietor who has a legal claim, when a peasant can tell us the history of each bit of land for ten leagues around? Above all, how make him believe that it is useful for the nation that Mr. So-and-So keeps a piece of land for his park when so many neighboring peasants would be only too glad to cultivate it?

And, lastly, how make the worker in a factory, or the miner in a mine, believe that factory and mine equitably belong to their present masters, when worker and even miner are beginning to see clearly through Panama scandals, bribery, French, Turkish or other railways, pillage of the State and legal theft, from which great commercial and industrial property are derived?

In fact the masses have never believed in sophisms taught by economists, uttered more to confirm exploiters in their rights than to convert exploited! Peasants and workers, crushed by misery and finding no support in the well-to-do classes, have let things go, save from time to time when they have affirmed their rights by insurrection. And if workers ever thought that the day would come when personal appropriation of capital would profit all by turning it into a stock of wealth to be shared by all, this illusion is vanishing like so many others. The worker perceives that he has been disinherited, and that disinherited he will remain, unless he has recourse to strikes or revolts to tear from his masters the smallest part of riches built up by his own efforts; that is to say, in order to get that little, he already must impose on himself the pangs of hunger and face imprisonment, if not exposure to Imperial, Royal, or Republican fusillades.

But a greater evil of the present system becomes more and more marked; namely, that in a system based on private appropriation, all that is necessary to life and to production—land, housing, food and tools—having once passed into the hands of a few, the production of necessities that would give well-being to all is continually hampered. The worker feels vaguely that our present technical power could give abundance to all, but he also perceives how the capitalistic system and the State hinder the conquest of this well-being in every way.

Far from producing more than is needed to assure material riches, we do not produce enough. When a peasant covets the parks and gardens of industrial filibusters and Panamists, round which judges and police mount guard—when he dreams of covering them with crops which, he knows, would carry abundance to the villages whose inhabitants feed on bread hardly washed down with sloe wine—he understands this.

The miner, forced to be idle three days a week, thinks of the tons of coal he might extract, and which are sorely needed in poor households.

The worker whose factory is closed, and who tramps the streets in search of work, sees bricklayers out of work like himself, while one-fifth of the population of Paris live in unsanitary hovels; he hears shoe-makers complain of want of work, while so many people need shoes—and so on.

In short, if certain economists delight in writing treatises on over-production, and in explaining each industrial crisis by this cause, they would be much at a loss if called upon to name a single article produced by France in greater quantities than are necessary to satisfy the needs of the whole population. It is certainly not corn: the country is obliged to import it. It is not wine either: peasants drink but little wine, and substitute sloe wine in its stead, and the inhabitants of towns have to be content with adulterated stuff. It is evidently not houses: millions still live in cottages of the most wretched description, with one or two apertures. It is not even good or bad books, for they are still objects of luxury in the villages. Only one thing is produced in quantities greater than needed—it is the budget-devouring individual; but such merchandise is not mentioned in lectures by political economists, although those individuals possess all the attributes of merchandise, being ever ready to sell themselves to the highest bidder.

What economists call over-production is but a production that is above the purchasing power of the worker, who is reduced to poverty by Capital and State. Now, this sort of over-production remains fatally characteristic of the present capitalist production, because— Proudhon has already shown it—workers cannot buy with their salaries what they have produced and at the same time copiously nourish the swarm of idlers who live upon their work.

The very essence of the present economic system is that the worker can never enjoy the well-being he has produced, and that the number of those who live at his expense will always augment. The more a country is advanced in industry, the more this number grows. Inevitably, industry is directed, and will have to be directed, not towards what is needed to satisfy the needs of all, but towards that which, at a given moment, brings in the greatest temporary profit to a few. Of necessity, the abundance of some will be based on the poverty of others, and the straitened circumstances of the greater number will have to be maintained at all costs, that there may be hands to sell themselves for a part only of that which they are capable of producing; without which, private accumulation of capital is impossible!

These characteristics of our economical system are its very essence. Without them, it cannot exist; for, who would sell his labor power for less than it is capable of bringing in, if he were not forced thereto by the threat of hunger?

And those essential traits of the system are also its most crushing condemnation.

As long as England and France were pioneers of industry, in the midst of nations backward in their technical development, and as long as neighbors purchased their wools, their cotton goods, their silks, their iron and machines, as well as a whole range of articles of luxury, at a price that allowed them to enrich themselves at the expense of their clients, the worker could be buoyed up by hope that he, too, would be called upon to appropriate an ever and ever larger share of the booty to himself. But these conditions are disappearing. In their turn, the backward nations of thirty years ago have become great producers of cotton goods, wools, silks, machines and articles of luxury. In certain branches of industry they have even taken the lead, and not only do they struggle with the pioneers of industry and commerce in distant lands, but they even compete with those pioneers in their own countries. In a few years Germany, Switzerland, Italy, the United States, Russia and Japan have become great industrial countries. Mexico, the Indies, even Serbia, are on the march—and what will it be when China begins to imitate Japan in manufacturing for the world's market?

The result is that industrial crises, the frequency and duration of which are always augmenting, have passed into a chronic state in many industries. Likewise, wars for Oriental and African markets have become the order of the day since several years; it is now twenty-five years that the sword of war has been suspended over European states. And if war has not burst forth, it is especially due to influential financiers who find it advantageous that States should become more and more indebted. But the day on which Money will find its interest in fomenting war, human flocks will be driven against other human flocks, and will butcher one another to settle the affairs of the world's master-financiers.

All is linked, all holds together under the present economic system, and all tends to make the fall of the industrial and mercantile system under which we live inevitable. Its duration is but a question of time that may already be counted by years and no longer by centuries. A question of time—and energetic attack on our part! Idlers do not make history: they suffer it!

That is why such powerful minorities constitute themselves in the midst of civilized nations, and loudly ask for the return to the community of all riches accumulated by the work of preceding generations. The holding in common of land, mines, factories, inhabited houses, and means of transport is already the watch-word of these imposing fractions, and repression—the favorite weapon of the rich and powerful—can no longer do anything to arrest the triumphal march of the spirit of revolt. And if millions of workers do not rise to seize the land and factories from the monopolists by force, be sure it is not for want of desire. They but wait for a favorable opportunity, a chance, such as presented itself in 1848, when they will be able to start the destruction of the present economic system, with the hope of being supported by an International movement.

That time cannot be long in coming; for since the International was crushed by governments in 1872—especially since then—it has made immense progress of which its most ardent partisans are hardly aware. It is, in fact, constituted in ideas, in sentiments, in the establishment of constant intercommunication. It is true the French, English, Italian and German plutocrats are so many rivals, and at any moment can even cause nations to war with one another. Nevertheless, be sure when the Communist and Social Revolution does take place in France, France will find the same sympathies as formerly among the nations of the world, including Germans, Italians and English. And when Germany, which, by the way, is nearer a revolution than is thought, will plant the flag—unfortunately a Jacobin one—of this revolution, when it will throw itself into the revolution with all the ardor of youth in an ascendant period, such as it is traversing today, it will find on this side of the Rhine all the sympathies and all the support of a nation that loves the audacity of revolutionists and hates the arrogance of plutocracy.

Diverse causes have up till now delayed the bursting forth of this inevitable revolution. The possibility of a great European war is no doubt partly answerable for it. But there is, it seems to me, another cause, a deeper-rooted one, to which I would call your attention. There is going on just now among the Socialists—many tokens lead us to believe it—a great transformation in ideas, like the one I sketched at the beginning of this lecture in speaking of general sciences. And the uncertainty of Socialists themselves concerning the organization of the society they are wishing for, paralyses their energy up to a certain point.

At the beginning, in the forties, Socialism presented itself as Communism, as a republic one and indivisible, as a governmental and Jacobin dictatorship, in its application to economics. Such was the ideal of that time. Religious and freethinking Socialists were equally ready to submit to any strong government, even an imperial one, if that government would only remodel economic relations to the worker's advantage.

A profound revolution has since been accomplished, especially among Latin and English peoples. Governmental Communism, like theocratic Communism, is repugnant to the worker. And this repugnance gave rise to a new conception or doctrine—that of Collectivism—in the International. This doctrine at first signified the llective possession of the instruments of production (not including what is necessary to live), and the right of each group to accept such method of remuneration, whether communistic or individualistic, as pleased its members. Little by little, however, this system was transformed into a sort of compromise between communistic and individualistic wage remuneration. Today the Collectivist wants all that belongs to production to become common property, but that each should be individually remunerated by labor checks, according to the number of hours he has spent in production. These checks would serve to buy all merchandise in the Socialist stores at cost price, which price would also be estimated in hours of labor.

But if you analyze this idea you will own that its essence, as summed up by one of our friends, is reduced to this:

Partial Communism in the possession of instruments of production and education.

Competition among individuals and groups for bread, housing and clothing.

Individualism for works of art and thought.

The Socialistic State's aid for children, invalids and old people.

In a word—a struggle for the means of existence mitigated by charity. Always the Christian maxim: "Wound to heal afterwards!" And always the door open to inquisition, in order to know if you are a man who must be left to struggle, or a man the State must succor.

The idea of labor checks, you know, is old. It dates from Robert Owen; Proudhon commended it in 1848; Marxists have made "Scientific Socialism" of it today.

We must say, however, that this system seems to have little hold on the minds of the masses; it would seem they foresaw its drawbacks, not to say its impossibility. Firstly, the duration of time given to any work does not give the measure of social utility of the work accomplished, and the theories of value that economists have endeavored to base, from Adam Smith to Marx, only on the cost of production, valued in labor time, have not solved the question of value. As soon as there is exchange, the value of an article becomes a complex quantity, and depends also on the degree of satisfaction which it brings to the needs—not of the individual, as certain economists stated formerly, but of the whole of society, taken in its entirety. Value is a social fact. Being the result of an exchange, it has a double aspect: that of labor, and that of satisfaction of needs, both evidently conceived in their social and not individual aspect.

On the other hand, when we analyze the evils of the present economic system, we see—and the worker knows it full well—that their essence lies in the forced necessity of the worker to sell his labor power. Not having the wherewithal to live for the next fortnight, and being prevented by the State from using his labor power without selling it to someone, the worker sells himself to the one who undertakes to give him work; he renounces the benefits his labor might bring him in; he abandons the lion's share of what he produces to his employer; he even abdicates his liberty; he renounces his right to make his opinion heard on the utility of what he is about to produce and on the way of producing it.

Thus results the accumulation of capital, not in its faculty of absorbing surplus-value, but in the forced position the worker is placed to sell his labor power: the seller being sure in advance that he will not receive all that his strength can produce, of being wounded in his interests, and of becoming the inferior of the buyer. Without this the capitalist would never have tried to buy him; which proves that to change the system it must be attacked in its essence: in its cause—sale and purchase—not in its effect—Capitalism.

Workers themselves have a vague intuition of this, and we hear them say oftener and oftener that nothing will be done if the Social Revolution does not begin with the distribution of products, if it does not guarantee the necessities of life to all—that is to say, housing, food and clothing. And we know that to do this is quite impossible, with the powerful means of production at our disposal.

If the worker continues to be paid in wages, he necessarily will remain the slave or the subordinate of the one to whom he is forced to sell his labor force—be the buyer a private individual or the State. In the popular mind—in that sum total of thousands of opinions crossing the human brain—it is felt that if the State were to be substituted for the employer, in his role of buyer and overseer of labor, it would still be an odious tyranny. A man of the people does not reason about abstractions, he thinks in concrete terms, and that is why he feels that the abstraction, the State, would for him assume the form of numberless functionaries, taken from among his factory and workshop comrades, and he knows what importance he can attach to their virtues: excellent comrades today, they become unbearable foremen tomorrow. And he looks for a social constitution that will eliminate the present evils without creating new ones.

That is why Collectivism has never taken hold of the masses, who always come back to Communism—but a Communism more and more stripped of the Jacobin theocracy and authoritarianism of the forties—to Free Communism—Anarchy.

Nay more: in calling to mind all we have seen during this quarter of a century in the European Socialist movement, I cannot help believing that modern Socialism is forced to make a step towards Free Communism; and that so long as that step is not taken, the incertitude in the popular mind that I have just pointed out will paralyze the efforts of Socialist propaganda.

Socialists seem to me to be brought, by force of circumstances, to recognize that the material guarantee of existence of all the members of the community shall be the first act of the Social Revolution.

But they are also driven to take another step. They are obliged to recognize that this guarantee must come, not from the State, but independently of the State, and without its intervention.

We have already obtained the unanimous assent of those who have studied the subject, that a society, having recovered the possession of all riches accumulated in its midst, can liberally assure abundance to all in return for four or five hours effective and manual work a day, as far as regards production. If everybody, from childhood, learned whence came the bread he eats, the house he dwells in, the book he studies, and so on; and if each one accustomed himself to complete mental work by manual labor in some branch of manufacture, society could easily perform this task, to say nothing of the further simplification of production which a more or less near future has in store for us.

In fact, it suffices to recall for a moment the present terrible waste, to conceive what a civilized society can produce with but a small quantity of labor if all share in it, and what grand works might be undertaken that are out of the question today. Unfortunately, the metaphysics called political economy has never troubled about that which should have been its essence—economy of labor.

There is no longer any doubt as regards the possibility of wealth in a Communist society, armed with our present machinery and tools.

Doubts only arise when the question at issue is, whether a society can exist in which man's actions are not subject to State control; whether, to reach well-being, it is not necessary for European communities to sacrifice the little personal liberty they have reconquered at the cost of so many sacrifices during this century? A section of Socialists believe that it is impossible to attain such a result without sacrificing personal liberty on the altar of the State. Another section, to which we belong, believes, on the contrary, that it is only by the abolition of the State, by the conquest of perfect liberty by the individual, by free agreement, association, and absolute free federation that we can reach Communism—the possession in common of our social inheritance, and the production in common of all riches.

That is the question outweighing all others at present, and Socialism must solve it, on pain of seeing all its efforts endangered and all its ulterior development paralysed.

Let us, therefore, analyse it with all the attention it deserves.

If every Socialist will carry his thoughts back to an earlier date, he will no doubt remember the host of prejudices aroused in him when, for the first time, he came to the idea that abolishing the capitalist system and private appropriation of land and capital had become an historical necessity.

The same feelings are today produced in the man who for the first time hears that the abolition of the State, its laws, its entire system of management, governmentalism and centralization, also becomes an historical necessity: that the abolition of the one without the abolition of the other is materially impossible. Our whole education—made, be it noted, by Church and State, in the interests of both—revolts at this conception.

Is it less true for that? And shall we allow our belief in the State to survive the host of prejudices we have already sacrificed for our emancipation?

It is not my intention to criticise tonight the State. That has been done and redone so often, and I am obliged to put off to another lecture the analysis of the historical part played by the State. A few general remarks will suffice.

To begin with, if man, since his origin, has always lived in societies, the State is but one of the forms of social life, quite recent as far as regards European societies. Men lived thousands of years before the first States were constituted; Greece and Rome existed for centuries before the Macedonian and Roman Empires were built up, and for us modern Europeans the centralized States date but from the sixteenth century. It was only then, after the defeat of the free mediæval Communes had been completed, that the mutual insurance company between military, judicial, landlord, and capitalist authority which we call "State," could be fully established.

It was only in the sixteenth century that a mortal blow was dealt to ideas of local independence, to free union and organization, to federation of all degrees among sovereign groups, possessing all functions now seized upon by the State. It was only then that the alliance between Church and the nascent power of Royalty put an end to an organization, based on the principle of federation, which had existed from the ninth to the fifteenth century, and which had produced in Europe the great period of free cities of the middle ages, whose character has been so well understood in France by Sismondi and Augustin Thierry—two historians unfortunately too little read now-a-days.

We know well the means by which this association of the lord, priest, merchant, judge, soldier, and king founded its domination. It was by the annihilation of all free unions: of village communities, guilds, trades unions, fraternities, and mediæval cities. It was by confiscating the land of the communes and the riches of the guilds; it was by the absolute and ferocious prohibition of all kinds of free agreement between men; it was by massacre, the wheel, the gibbet, the sword, and the fire that Church and State established their domination, and that they succeeded henceforth to reign over an incoherent agglomeration of subjects, who had no direct union more among themselves.

It is now hardly thirty or forty years ago that we began to reconquer, by struggle, by revolt, the first steps of the right of association, that was freely practised by the artisans and the tillers of the soil through the whole of the middle ages.

And, already now, Europe is covered by thousands of voluntary associations for study and teaching, for industry, commerce, science, art, literature, exploitation, resistance to exploitation, amusement, serious work, gratification and self-denial, for all that makes up the life of an active and thinking being. We see these societies rising in all nooks and corners of all domains: political, economic, artistic, intellectual. Some are as short-lived as roses, some hold their own since several decades, and all strive—while maintaining the independence of each group, circle, branch, or section—to federate, to unite, across frontiers as well as among each nation; to cover all the life of civilized men with a net, meshes of which are intersected and interwoven. Their numbers can already be reckoned by tens of thousands, they comprise millions of adherents—although less than fifty years have elapsed since Church and State began to tolerate a few of them—very few, indeed.

These societies already begin to encroach everywhere on the functions of the State, and strive to substitute free action of volunteers for that of a centralized State. In England we see arise insurance companies against theft, societies for coast defense, volunteer societies for land defense, which the State endeavors to get under its thumb, thereby making them instruments of domination, although their original aim was to do without the State. Were it not for Church and State, free societies would have already conquered the whole of the immense domain of education. And, in spite of all difficulties, they begin to invade this domain as well, and make their influence already felt.

And when we mark the progress already accomplished in that direction, in spite of and against the State, which tries by all means to maintain its supremacy of recent origin; when we see how voluntary societies invade everything and are only impeded in their development by the State, we are forced to recognize a powerful tendency, a latent force in modern society. And we ask ourselves this question: If, five, ten, or twenty years hence—it matters little—the workers succeed by revolt in destroying the said mutual insurance society of landlords, bankers, priests, judges, and soldiers; if the people become masters of their destiny for a few months, and lay hands on the riches they have created, and which belong to them by right—will they really begin to reconstitute that blood-sucker, the State? Or will they not rather try to organize from the simple to the complex according to mutual agreement and to the infinitely varied, ever-changing needs of each locality, in order to secure the possession of those riches for themselves, to mutually guarantee one another's life, and to produce what will be found necessary for life?

Will they follow the dominant tendency of the century, towards decentralization, home rule and free agreement; or will they march contrary to this tendency and strive to reconstitute demolished authority?

Educated men—"civilized," as Fourier used to say with disdain—tremble at the idea that society might some day be without judges, police, or gaolers.

But, frankly, do you need them as much as you have been told in musty books? Books written, be it noted, by scientists who generally know well what has been written before them, but, for the most part, absolutely ignore the people and their every-day life.

If we can wander, without fear, not only in the streets of Paris, which bristle with police, but especially in rustic walks where you rarely meet passers by, is it to the police that we owe this security? Or rather to the absence of people who care to rob or murder us? I am evidently not speaking of the one who carries millions about him. That one—a recent trial tells us—is soon robbed, by preference in places where there are as many policemen as lamp posts. No, I speak of the man who fears for his life and not for his purse filled with ill-gotten sovereigns. Are his fears real?

Besides, has not experience demonstrated quite recently that Jack the Ripper performed his exploits under the eye of the London police—a most active force—and that he only left off killing when the population of Whitechapel itself began to give chase to him?

And in our every-day relations with our fellow-citizens, do you think that it is really judges, gaolers, and police that hinder anti-social acts from multiplying? The judge, ever ferocious, because he is a maniac of law, the accuser, the informer, the police spy, all those interlopers that live from hand to mouth around the Law Courts, do they not scatter demoralization far and wide into society? Read the trials, glance behind the scenes, push your analysis further than the exterior facade of law courts, and you will come out sickened.

Have not prisons—which kill all will and force of character in man, which enclose within their walls more vices than are met with on any other spot of the globe—always been universities of crime? Is not the court of a tribunal a school of ferocity? And so on.

When we ask for the abolition of the State and its organs we are always told that we dream of a society composed of men better than they are in reality. But no; a thousand times, no. All we ask is that men should not be made worse than they are, by such institutions!

Once a German jurist of great renown, Ihering, wanted to sum up the scientific work of his life and write a treatise, in which he proposed to analyze the factors that preserve social life in society. *Purpose in Law* (*Der Zweck im Rechte*), such is the title of that book, which enjoys a well-deserved reputation.

He made an elaborate plan of his treatise, and, with much erudition, discussed both coercive factors which are used to maintain society: wagedom and the different forms of coercion which are sanctioned by law. At the end of his work he reserved two paragraphs only to mention the two non-coercive factors — the feeling of duty and the feeling of mutual sympathy — to which he attached little importance, as might be expected from a writer in law.

But what happened? As he went on analyzing the coercive factors he realized their insufficiency. He consecrated a whole volume to their analysis, and the result was to lessen their importance! When he began the last two paragraphs, when he began to reflect upon the non-coercive factors of society, he perceived, on the contrary, their immense, outweighing importance; and instead of two paragraphs, he found himself obliged to write a second volume, twice as large as the first, on these two factors: voluntary restraint and mutual help; and yet, he analyzed but an infinitesimal part of these latter — those which result from personal sympathy — and hardly touched free agreement, which results from social institutions.

Well, then, leave off repeating the formulæ which you have learned at school; meditate on this subject; and the same thing that happened to Ihering will happen to you: you will recognize the infinitesimal importance of coersion, as compared to the voluntary assent, in society.

On the other hand, if by following the very old advice given by Bentham you begin to think of the fatal consequences — direct, and especially indirect — of legal coersion, like Tolstoy, like us, you will begin to hate use of coersion, and you will begin to say that society possesses a thousand other means for preventing antisocial acts. If it neglects those means today, it is because, being educated by Church and State, our cowardice and apathy of spirit hinder us seeing clearly on this point. When a child has committed a fault, it is so easy to hang a man — especially when there is an executioner who is paid so much for each execution — and it dispenses us from thinking of the cause of crimes.

It is often said that Anarchists live in a world of dreams to come, and do not see the things which happen today. We do see them only too well, and in their true colors, and that is what makes us carry the hatchet into the forest of prejudice that besets us.

Far from living in a world of visions and imagining men better than they are, we see them as they are; and that is why we affirm that the best of men is made essentially bad by the exercise of authority, and that the theory of the "balancing of powers" and "control of authorities" is a hypocritical formula, invented by those who have seized power, to make the "sovereign people," whom they despise, believe that the people themselves are governing. It is because we know men that we say to those who imagine that men would devour one another without those governors: "You reason like the king, who, being sent across the frontier, called out, 'What will become of my poor subjects without me?'"

Ah, if men were those superior beings that the utopians of authority like to speak to us of, if we could close our eyes to reality, and live, like them, in a world of dreams and illusions as to the superiority of those who think themselves called to power, perhaps we also should do like them; perhaps we also should believe in the virtues of those who govern.

With virtuous masters, what dangers could slavery offer? Do you remember the slave-owner of whom we heard so often, hardly thirty years ago? Was he not supposed to take paternal care of his slaves? "He alone," we were told, "could hinder these lazy, indolent, improvident children dying of hunger. How could he crush his slaves through hard labor, or mutilate them by blows, when his own interest lay in feeding them well, in taking care of them as much as of his own children! And then, did not 'the law' see to it that the least swerving of a slave-owner from the path of duty was punished?" How many times have we not been told so! But the reality was such that, having returned from a voyage to Brazil, Darwin was haunted all his life by the cries of agony of mutilated slaves, by the sobs of moaning women whose fingers were crushed in thumbscrews!

If the gentlemen in power were really so intelligent and so devoted to the public cause, as panegyrists of authority love to represent, what a pretty government and paternal utopia we should be able to construct! The employer would never be the tyrant of the worker; he would be the father! The factory would be a palace of delight, and never would masses of workers be doomed to physical deterioration. The State would not poison its workers by making matches with white phosphorus, for which it is so easy to substitute red phosphorus. A judge would not have the ferocity to condemn the wife and children of the one whom he sends to prison to suffer years of hunger and misery and to die some day of anemia; never would a public prosecutor ask for the head of the accused for the unique pleasure of showing off his oratorical talent; and nowhere would we find a gaoler or an executioner to do the bidding of judges, who have not the courage to carry out their sentences themselves. What do I say! We should never have enough Plutarchs to praise the virtues of Members of Parliament who would all hold Panama checks in horror! Biribi would become an austere nursery of virtue, and permanent armies would be the joy of citizens, as soldiers would only take up arms to parade before nursemaids, and to carry nosegays on the point of their bayonets!

Oh, the beautiful utopia, the lovely Christmas dream we can make as soon as we admit that those who govern represent a superior caste, and have hardly any or no knowledge of simple mortals' weaknesses! It would then suffice to make them control one another in hierarchical fashion, to let them exchange fifty papers, at most, among different administrators, when the wind blows down a tree on the national road. Or, if need be, they would have only to be valued at their proper worth, during elections, by those same masses of mortals which are supposed to be endowed with all stupidity in their mutual relations but become wisdom itself when they have to elect their masters.

All the science of government, imagined by those who govern, is imbibed with these utopias. But we know men too well to dream such dreams. We have not two measures for the virtues of the governed and those of the governors; we know that we ourselves are not without faults and that the best of us would soon be corrupted by the exercise of power. We take men for what they are worth—and that is why we hate the government of man by man, and that we work with all our might—perhaps not strong enough—to put an end to it.

But it is not enough to destroy. We must also know how to build, and it is owing to not having thought about it that the masses have always been led astray in all their revolutions. After having demolished they abandoned the care of reconstruction to the middle class people, who possessed a more or less precise conception of what they wished to realize, and who consequently reconstituted authority to their own advantage.

That is why Anarchy, when it works to destroy authority in all its aspects, when it demands the abrogation of laws and the abolition of the mechanism that serves to impose them, when it refuses all hierarchical organization and preaches free agreement—at the same time strives to maintain and enlarge the precious kernel of social customs without which no human or animal society can exist. Only, instead of demanding that those social customs should be maintained through the authority of a few, it demands it from the continued action of all.

Communist customs and institutions are of absolute necessity for society, not only to solve economic difficulties, but also to maintain and develop social customs that bring men in contact with one another; they must be looked to for establishing such relations between men that the interest of each should be the interest of all; and this alone can unite men instead of dividing them.

In fact, when we ask ourselves by what means a certain moral level can be maintained in a human or animal society, we find only three such means: the repression of anti-social acts; moral teaching; and the practice of mutual help itself. And as all three have already been put to the test of practice, we can judge them by their effects.

As to the impotence of repression—it is sufficiently demonstrated by the disorder of present society and by the necessity of a revolution that we all desire or feel inevitable. In the domain of economy, coercion has led us to industrial servitude; in the domain of politics—to the State, that is to say—to the destruction of all ties that formerly existed among citizens, and to the nation becoming nothing but an incoherent mass of obedient subjects of a central authority.

Not only has a coercive system contributed and powerfully aided to create all the present economical, political and social evils, but it has given proof of its absolute impotence to raise the moral level of societies; it has not been even able to maintain it at the level it had already reached. If a benevolent fairy could only reveal to our eyes all the crimes that are committed every day, every minute, in a civilized society under cover of the unknown, or the protection of law itself—society would shudder at that terrible state of affairs. The authors of the greatest political crimes, like those of Napoleon III's *coup d'etat*, or the bloody week in May after the fall of the Commune of 1871, never are arraigned; and as a poet said; "the small miscreants are punished for the satisfaction of the great ones." More than that, when authority takes the moralization of society in hand, by "punishing criminals" it only heaps up new crimes!

Practised for centuries, repression has so badly succeeded that it has but led us into a blind alley from which we can only issue by carrying torch and hatchet into the institutions of our authoritarian past.

Far be it from us not to recognize the importance of the second factor, moral teaching—especially that which is unconsciously transmitted in society and results from the whole of the ideas and comments emitted by each of us on facts and events of every-day life. But this force can only act on society under one condition, that of not being crossed by a mass of contradictory immoral teachings resulting from the practice of institutions.

In that case its influence is nil or baneful. Take Christian morality: what other teaching could have had more hold on minds than that spoken in the name of a crucified God, and could have acted with all its mystical force, all its poetry of martyrdom, its grandeur in forgiving executioners? And yet the institution was more powerful than the religion: soon Christianity—a revolt against imperial Rome— was conquered by that same Rome; it accepted its maxims, customs, and language. The Christian church accepted the Roman law as its own, and as such—allied to the State—it became in history the most furious enemy of all semi-communist institutions, to which Christianity appealed at its origin.

Can we for a moment believe that moral teaching, patronized by circulars from ministers of public instruction, would have the creative force that Christianity has not had? And what could the verbal teaching of truly social men do, if it were counteracted by the whole teaching derived from institutions based, as our present institutions of property and State are, upon unsocial principles?

The third element alone remains—the institution itself, acting in such a way as to make social acts a state of habit and instinct. This element—history proves it—has never missed its aim, never has it acted as a double-bladed sword; and its influence has only been weakened when custom strove to become immovable, crystallized, to become in its turn a religion not to be questioned when it endeavored to absorb the individual, taking all freedom of action from him and compelling him to revolt against that which had become, through its crystallization, an enemy to progress.

In fact, all that was an element of progress in the past or an instrument of moral and intellectual improvement of the human race is due to the practice of mutual aid, to the customs that recognized the equality of men and brought them to ally, to unite, to associate for the purpose of producing and consuming, to unite for purpose of defence, to federate and to recognize no other judges in fighting out their differences than the arbitrators they took from their own midst.

Each time these institutions, issued from popular genius, when it had reconquered its liberty for a moment—each time these institutions developed in a new direction, the moral level of society, its material well-being, its liberty, its intellectual progress, and the affirmation of individual originality made a step in advance. And, on the contrary, each time that in the course of history, whether following upon a foreign conquest, or whether by developing authoritarian prejudices men become more and more divided into governors and governed, exploiters and exploited, the moral level fell, the well-being of the masses decreased in order to insure riches to a few, and the spirit of the age declined.

History teaches us this, and from this lesson we have learned to have confidence in free Communist institutions to raise the moral level of societies, debased by the practice of authority.

Today we live side by side without knowing one another. We come together at meetings on an election day: we listen to the lying or fanciful professions of faith of a candidate, and we return home. The State has the care of all questions of public interest; the State alone has the function of seeing that we do not harm the interests of our neighbor, and, if it fails in this, of punishing us in order to repair the evil.

Our neighbor may die of hunger or murder his children—it is no business of ours; it is the business of the policeman. You hardly know one another, nothing unites you, everything tends to alienate you from one another, and finding no better way, you ask the Almighty (formerly it was a God, now it is the State) to do all that lies within his power to stop anti-social passions from reaching their highest climax.

In a Communist society such estrangement, such confidence in an outside force could not exist. Communist organization cannot be left to be constructed by legislative bodies called parliaments, municipal or communal council. It must be the work of all, a natural growth, a product of the constructive genius of the great mass. Communism cannot be imposed from above; it could not live even for a few months if the constant and daily co-operation of all did not uphold it. It must be free.

It cannot exist without creating a continual contact between all for the thousands and thousands of common transactions; it cannot exist without creating local life, independent in the smallest unities — the block of houses, the street, the district, the commune. It would not answer its purpose if it did not cover society with a network of thousands of associations to satisfy its thousand needs: the necessaries of life, articles of luxury, of study, enjoyment, amusements. And such associations cannot remain narrow and local; they must necessarily tend (as is already the case with learned societies, cyclist clubs, humanitarian societies and the like) to become international.

And the sociable customs that Communism — were it only partial at its origin — must inevitably engender in life, would already be a force incomparably more powerful to maintain and develop the kernel of sociable customs than all repressive machinery.

This, then, is the form — sociable institution — of which we ask the development of the spirit of harmony that Church and State had undertaken to impose on us — with the sad result we know only too well. And these remarks contain our answer to those who affirm that Communism and Anarchy cannot go together. They are, you see, a necessary complement to one another. The most powerful development of individuality, or individual originality — as one of our comrades has so well said — can only be produced when the first needs of food and shelter are satisfied; when the struggle for existence against the forces of nature has been simplified; when man's time is no longer taken up entirely by the meaner side of daily subsistence — then only, his intelligence, his artistic taste, his inventive spirit, his genius, can develop freely and ever strive to greater achievements.

Communism is the best basis for individual development and freedom; not that individualism which drives man to the war of each against all — this is the only one known up till now — but that which represents the full expansion of man's faculties, the superior development of what is original in him, the greatest fruitfulness of intelligence, feeling and will.

Such being our ideal, what does it matter to us that it cannot be realized at once!

Our first duty is to find out, by an analysis of society, its characteristic tendencies at a given moment of evolution and to state them clearly. Then, to act according to those tendencies in our relations with all those who think as we do. And, finally, from today and especially daring a revolutionary period, work for the destruction of the institutions, as well as the prejudices, that impede the development of such tendencies.

That is all we can do by peaceable or revolutionary methods, and we know that by favoring those tendencies we contribute to progress, while who resist them impede the march of progress.

Nevertheless, men often speak of stages to be traveled through, and they propose to work to reach what they consider to be the nearest station and only then to take the high road leading to what they recognize to be a still higher ideal.

But reasoning like this seems to me to misunderstand the true character of human progress and to make use of a badly chosen military comparison. Humanity is not a rolling ball, nor even a marching column. It is a whole that evolves simultaneously in the multitude of millions of which it is composed; and if you wish for a comparison, you must rather take it in the laws of organic evolution than in those of an inorganic moving body.

The fact is that each phase of development of a society is a resultant of all the activities of the intellects which compose that society; it bears the imprint of all those millions of wills. Consequently, whatever may be the stage of development that the twentieth century is preparing for us, this future state of society will show the effects of the awakening of libertarian ideas which is now taking place. And the depth with which this movement will be impressed upon the coming twentieth century institutions will depend upon the number of men who will have broken today with authoritarian prejudices, on the energy they will have used in attacking old institutions, on the impression they will make on the masses, on the clearness with which the ideal of a free society will have been impressed on the minds of the masses. But, today, we can say in full confidence that in France the awakening of libertarian ideas had already put its stamp on society; and that the next revolution will not be the Jacobin revolution which it would have been had it burnt out twenty years ago.

And as these ideas are neither the invention of a man nor a group, but result from the whole of the movement of ideas of the time, we can be sure that, whatever comes out of the next revolution, it will not be the dictatorial and centralized Communism which was so much in vogue forty years ago, nor the authoritarian Collectivism to which we were quite recently invited to ally ourselves, and which its advocates dare only defend very feebly at present.

The "first stage," it is certain, will then be quite different from what was described under that name hardly twenty years ago. The latest developments of the libertarian ideas have already modified it beforehand in an Anarchist sense.

I have already mentioned that the great all-dominating question now is for the Socialist party, taken as a whole, to harmonize its ideal of society with the libertarian movement that germinates, in the spirit of the masses, in literature, in science, in philosophy. It is also, it is especially so, to rouse the spirit of popular initiative.

Now, it is precisely the workers' and peasants' initiative that all parties—the Socialist authoritarian party included—have always stifled, wittingly or not, by party discipline. Committees, centers, ordering everything; local organs having but to obey, "so as not to put the unity of the organization in danger." A whole teaching, in a word; a whole false history, written to serve that purpose, a whole incomprehensible pseudo-science of economics, elaborated to this end.

Well, then, those who will work to break up these superannuated tactics, those who will know how to rouse the spirit of initiative in individuals and in groups, those who will be able to create in their mutual relations a movement and a life based on the principles of free understanding—those that will understand that variety, conflict even, is life, and that uniformity is death—they will work, not for future centuries, but in good earnest for the next revolution, for our own times.

We need not fear the dangers and "abuses" of liberty. It is only those who do nothing who make no mistakes. As to those who only know how to obey, they make just as many, and more, mistakes than those who strike out their own path in trying to act in the direction their intelligence and their social education suggest to them. The ideal of liberty of the individual—if it is incorrectly understood owing to surroundings where the notion of solidarity is insufficiently accentuated by institutions—can certainly lead isolated men to acts that are repugnant to the social sentiments of humanity. Let us admit that it does happen: is it, however, a reason for throwing the principle of liberty overboard? Is it a reason for accepting the teaching of those masters who, in order to prevent "digressions," re-establish the censure of an enfranchised press and guillotine, advanced parties to maintain uniformity and discipline—that which, when all is said, was in 1793 the best means of insuring the triumph of reaction?

The only thing to be done when we see anti-social acts committed in the name of liberty of the individual, is to repudiate the principle of "each for himself and God for all," and to have the courage to say aloud in anyone's presence what we think of such acts. This can perhaps bring about a conflict; but conflict is life itself. And from the conflict will arise an appreciation of those acts far more just than all those appreciations which could have been produced under the influence of old-established ideas.

When the moral level of a society descends to the point it has reached today we must expect beforehand that a revolt against such a society will sometimes assume forms that will make us shudder. No doubt, heads paraded on pikes disgust us; but the high and low gibbets of the old regime in France, and the iron cages Victor Hugo has told us of, were they not the origin of this bloody exhibition? Let us hope that the cold-blooded massacre of thirty-five thousand Parisians in May, 1871, after the fall of the Commune, and the bombardment of Paris by Thiers, will have passed over the French nation without leaving too great a fund of ferocity. Let us hope that. Let us also hope that the corruption of the swell mob, which is continually brought to light in recent trials, will not yet have ruined the heart of the nation. Let us hope it! Let us help that it be so! But if our hopes are not fulfilled—you, young Socialists, will you then turn your backs on the people in revolt, because the ferocity of the rulers of today will have left its furrow in the people's minds; because the mud from above has splashed far and wide?

It is evident that so profound a revolution producing itself in people's minds cannot be confined to the domain of ideas without expanding to the sphere of action. As was so well expressed by the sympathetic young philosopher, too early snatched by death from our midst, Mark Guyau, in one of the most beautiful books published for thirty years, there is no abyss between thought and action, at least for those who are not used to modern sophistry. Conception is already a beginning of action.

Consequently, the new ideas have provoked a multitude of acts of revolt in all countries, under all possible conditions: first, individual revolt against Capital and State; then collective revolt—strikes and working class insurrections—both preparing, in men's minds as in actions, a revolt of the masses, a revolution. In this, Socialism and Anarchism have only followed the course of evolution, which is always accomplished by force—ideas at the approach of great popular risings.

That is why it would be wrong to attribute the monopoly of acts of revolt to Anarchism. And, in fact, when we pass in review the acts of revolt of the last quarter of a century, we see them proceeding from all parties.

In all Europe we see a multitude of risings of working masses and peasants. Strikes, which were once "a war of folded arms," today easily turning to revolt, and sometimes taking—in the United States, in Belgium, in Andalusia—the proportions of vast insurrections. In the new and old worlds it is by the dozen that we count the risings of strikers having turned to revolts.

On the other hand, the individual act of revolt takes all possible characters, and all advanced parties contribute to it. We pass before us the rebel young woman Vera Zassulitch shooting a satrap of Alexander II; the Social Democrat Hœdel and the Republican Nobiling shooting at the Emperor of Germany; the cooper Otero shooting at the King of Spain, and the religious Mazzmian, Passanante, striking at the King of Italy. We see agrarian murders in Ireland and explosions in London, organized by Irish Nationalists who have a horror of Socialism and Anarchism. We see a whole generation of young Russians—Socialists, Constitutionalists and Jacobins—declare war to the knife against Alexander II, and pay for that revolt against autocracy by thirty-five executions and swarms of exiles. Numerous acts of personal revenge take place among Belgian,

English and American miners; and it is only at the end of this long series that we see the Anarchists appear with their acts of revolt in Spain and France.

And, during this same period, massacres, wholesale and retail, organized by governments, follow their regular course. To the applause of the European bourgeoisie, the Versailles Assembly causes thirty-five thousand Parisian workmen to be butchered — for the most part prisoners of the vanquished Commune. "Pinkerton thugs" — that private army of the rich American capitalists — massacre strikers according to the rules of that art. Priests incite an idiot to shoot at Louise Michel, who — as a true Anarchist — snatches her would-be murderer from his judges by pleading for him. Outside Europe the Indians of Canada are massacred and Riel is strangled, the Matabele are exterminated, Alexandria is bombarded, without saying more of the butcheries in Madagascar, in Tonkin, in Turkoman's land everywhere, to which is given the name of war. And, finally, each year hundreds and even thousands of years of imprisonment are distributed among the rebellious workers of the two continents, and the wives and children, who are thus condemned to expiate the so-called crimes of their fathers, are doomed to the darkest misery. The rebels are transported to Siberia, to Biribi, to Noumea and to Guiana; and in those places of exile the convicts are shot down like dogs for the least act of insubordination. What a terrible indictment the balance sheet of the sufferings endured by workers and their friends, during this last quarter of a century, would be! What a multitude of horrible details that are unknown to the public at large and that would haunt you like a nightmare if I ventured to tell you them tonight! What a fit of passion each page would provoke if the martyrology of the modern forerunners of the great Social Revolution were written! Well, then, we have lived through such a history, and each one of us has read whole pages from that book of blood and misery.

And, in the face of those sufferings, those executions, those Guianas, Siberias, Noumeas and Biribis, they have the insolence to reproach the rebel worker with want of respect for human life!!!

But the whole of our present life extinguishes the respect for human life! The judge who sentences to death, and his lieutenant, the executioner, who garrots in broad daylight in Madrid, or guillotines in the mists of Paris amid the jeers of the degraded members of high and low society; the general who massacres at Bac-leh, and the newspaper correspondent who strives to cover the assassins with glory; the employer who poisons his workmen with white lead, because—he answers—"it would cost so much more to substitute oxide of zinc for it;" the so-called English geographer who kills an old women lest she should awake a hostile village by her sobs, and the German geographer who causes the girl he had taken as a mistress to be hanged with her lover, the court-martial that is content with fifteen days arrest for the Biribi gaoler convicted of murder....all, all, all in the present society teaches absolute contempt for human life—for that flesh that costs so little in the market! And those who garrot, assassinate, who kill depreciated human merchandise, they who have made a religion of the maxim that for the safety of the public you must garrot, shoot and kill, they complain that human life is not sufficiently respected!!!

No, citizens, as long as society accepts the law of retaliation, as long as religion and law, the barrack and the law-courts, the prison and industrial penal servitude, the press and the school continue to teach supreme contempt for the life of the individual—do not ask the rebels against that society to respect it. It would be exacting a degree of gentleness and magnanimity from them, infinitely superior to that of the whole society.

If you wish, like us, that the entire liberty of the individual and, consequently, his life be respected, you are necessarily brought to repudiate the government of man by man, whatever shape it assumes; you are forced to accept the principles of Anarchy that you have spurned so long. You must then search with us the forms of society that can best realize that ideal and put an end to all the violence that rouses your indignation.

CPSIA information can be obtained
at www.ICGtesting.com
Printed in the USA
BVHW061314110221
599814BV00004B/706

9 781934 941812